MACARTNEY

The Greatest Words in the Bible and in Human Speech

Books by Clarence E. Macartney

Chariots of Fire
Great Women of the Bible
The Greatest Questions of the Bible and of Life
The Greatest Texts of the Bible
The Greatest Words in the Bible and in Human Speech
He Chose Twelve
Paul the Man
Strange Texts but Grand Truths
12 Great Questions About Christ

CLARENCE E. MACARTNEY

The Greatest Words in the Bible and in Human Speech

kregel
PUBLICATIONS

Grand Rapids, MI 49501

The Greatest Words in the Bible and in Human Speech
by Clarence E. Macartney.

Published in 1995 by Kregel Publications, a division of
Kregel, Inc., P.O. Box 2607, Grand Rapids, MI 49501.
Kregel Publications provides trusted, biblical publications
for Christian growth and service. Your comments and
suggestions are valued.

Cover Photo: Art Jacobs
Cover and book design: Alan G. Hartman

Library of Congress Cataloging-in-Publication Data
Macartney, Clarence Edward Noble, 1879–1957
   The greatest words in the Bible and in human speech /
Clarence E. Macartney.
     p.   cm.
   Originally published: Nashville: Cokesbury Press, c1938.
   1. Presbyterian Church—Sermons. 2. Sermons, American.
I. Title.
BX9178.M172G7 1995   252'.051—dc20   93–36682
                                       CIP

ISBN 0-8254-3271-5 (paperback)

1 2 3 4 5 Printing / Year 99 98 97 96 95

Printed in the United States of America

CONTENTS

FOREWORD

When first announced, the series on *The Greatest Words in the Bible and in Human Speech* was made up of only five sermons, but the quickly manifested popular interest in these words, and the joy and satisfaction in working out the sermons, led me to extend this series to the fifteen sermons that are incorporated in this volume.

I do not know when I have had more pleasure in writing and preaching a series of sermons, although from my first years in the ministry I have followed the plan of serial preaching, especially at the evening service. Once the word was selected, the sermon came easily and naturally, and the more so because the plan was to illustrate and demonstrate the truth concerning a given word by incidents in the lives of the men and women in the Bible. Such a series of sermons has thus a twofold advantage: the "Great Words" themselves are words that sweep all the chords of life; they stand for the great desires, fears, hopes, and emotions of men's hearts; and when they are made to echo in the lives of the men and women in the Bible, they are all the more stirring. This is the most effective kind of biblical preaching, the sore need of the church of our day.

If other ministers plan to preach a similar series of sermons, for I have by no means exhausted *The Greatest Words in the Bible and in Human Speech*, let me suggest that they take advantage, as I did, of a natural curiosity. It will be noted that in announcing the sermons, the particular word was never given, and even in the preaching of the sermon, the word was not spoken until well along in the introduction. This gives the preacher the advantage of a legitimate and natural curiosity and suspense.

But, best of all, the sermons on *The Greatest Words in the Bible and in Human Speech* give the preacher an opportunity to present in a new and fresh way the great truths of redemption from sin by our Savior Jesus Christ, to sweep the chords of the human heart, and to proclaim the length and the breadth and the depth and the height of the "Glorious Gospel of the Blessed God."

CLARENCE E. MACARTNEY

1

THE SADDEST WORD

What is the saddest word in the Bible and in human speech? Some thought that it was Death; others, Hell; others, Depart; and many voted for Lost. But what is the saddest word? What is the word that is the fountain of woe, the mother of sorrows, as universal as human nature, as eternal as human history? What is the word that is the cause of all war and violence and hatred and sorrow and pain? What is the word that is man's worst enemy? What is the word that nailed the Son of God to the Cross? That word is *sin*. "Sin croucheth at the door"—Genesis 4:7.

And there, ever since, with its sorrow and its woe, sin has been crouching at humanity's door, and will continue to crouch, until the world has been redeemed.

This is not the first appearance of sin, but the first mention of sin, and the first appearance of the final fruit of sin. "When lust hath conceived it bringeth forth sin, and sin when it is finished bringeth forth death." Here, then, you have death, the first murder, the first death of man, as the finished work of sin. This is the beginning of the long, sad chapter of sin, a chapter which comes to a close only with the last chapter of the Bible, when there shall be no more curse and no more sin. All the sorrow, all the woe, all the bitterness and violence and heartache and shame and tragedy between man's creation and fall and his final redemption and restoration to the image of God is summed up in that one word sin.

Lost is, indeed, a sad word; so sad that only Christ who came to seek and to save the lost would seem to have the right to pronounce it. But through what are men lost? Lost to themselves, and lost to God. They are lost through sin, and when we deal not with effects but with causes there is no doubt that sin is the saddest word.

Our plan is to show the sadness of sin, not by abstract argument or reasoning, but by illustration in the lives of men, by a recital of what sin did in the lives of men whose history is related in the Bible. The Bible is the perfect and eternal mirror of the human heart, and you can be sure that what sin did in the lives of men in the Bible it is doing in the lives of men today. What was true of man in Eden is true of man in Hollywood, and what was true of man in Jericho and Jerusalem is true of man in New York or Pittsburgh.

CAIN AND THE SADNESS OF SIN IN PERSONAL AND FAMILY LIFE

There was something wrong with Cain before he brought his offering, for God's displeasure and rejection of Cain's offering, and His acceptance of the offering of Abel, was not because of what Cain brought, the firstlings of the field, or what Abel brought, the first fruits of his flocks. The trouble was in the heart of Cain. God said to him, warning him, "If thou doest evil, sin croucheth at the door." This sin in the heart of Cain was quickly followed, for sin multiplies rapidly, by the sin of envy and hatred. For the first time in the history of mankind sin painted man's face with the dark colors of hatred and jealousy. Hate lifted its hand and the first murder was committed, and the blood of Abel cried for vengeance from the ground, stained for the first time, alas, not for the last, with the blood of man.

Here, at the very beginning of man's history, you have a powerful demonstration of the sorrow and havoc of sin in personal and family relationships. This was a brother who slew his brother. Life has its struggles and hardships and trials, but where love and loyalty light the way all things can be endured. The real bitterness and sadness are in the infidelities and cruelties of personal and family relationships. This is the real burden and load of life. Widen the circle and you come to the relationship of nations, for God hath made of one blood all nations of men, and wherever man kills man he kills a brother. From peaceful Majorca, and out of the incomparably blue sky, suddenly six planes appear in the heavens above populous Barcelona. As they float in ether, men in those planes pull a lever, and in a few minutes half a thousand are dead and mangled, hundreds more wounded, and thousands broken-hearted. What is the explanation? What is the explanation of those one hundred and fifty-three dead orphans lying among the slaughtered? What is it in man that produces so fearful a spectacle? Only one thing, sin.

SAUL AND THE SADNESS OF SIN IN THE HIGHLY GIFTED LIFE

There is always something likable and appealing in Saul. He draws you like a magnet across the ages. In many respects he was a great man, head and shoulders over all Israel, not only in stature, but in moral qualities, such as courage, patriotism, humility, and sincere affection. His choice for the first king of Israel seems well justified.

Then pride and disobedience, reliance upon himself instead of upon God, show themselves in his life, and when he has been rejected and another chosen in his place, then jealousy begins to rage in his heart. We behold him seeking to kill his son whom he loved, and David his best friend, who had charmed away with his lyre Saul's evil spirit. Then, abandoned by Samuel, rejected and forsaken by God, Saul goes at midnight to consult the witch and call up dishonored and neglected Samuel, who pronounces upon him tomorrow's doom, "Tomorrow shalt thou and thy sons be with me."

There you see what sin can do to a great and gifted life. No wonder Samuel wept all night over Saul and his fall, no wonder that David, in the most beautiful poem ever spoken by man, lamented over Saul, his shield and his bow vilely cast away as if he had not been anointed with oil. Sin spares none. It strikes at the highest and loves a shining mark. How often the story of Saul has been repeated, and men with preeminent gifts and notable talents have been broken, dishonored, and dethroned by sin.

DAVID AND THE SADNESS OF SIN IN THE GODLY MAN

David was a godly man, and his every natural impulse was Godward. That is true in spite of the ever repeated scoffing of ungodly men at the character of David. On one side of his life he was, indeed, a man after God's own heart. That was spoken of David, remember, before his fall, not after it.

When David ought to have been at the head of his army, which was abroad in a distant campaign, he remained at home. Taking his ease one night on the roof garden of his palace, he saw a beautiful woman and was enamored of her and took her for his own. That was not the first nor the last time that such a thing has happened. But David's first sin was followed by something much worse, the cruel and treacherous murder of the woman's husband, and David's loyal officer in the army. That is the story of David's fall.

Now, who is this that we see prostrate in the dust? And whose cries of penitential confession are these that we hear? Who is this that beseeches God not to cast him away from His presence, and not to take His Holy Spirit from him? David, is it thou? Thou, the ruddy youth who kept the sheep on the hillside, the youth who slew both the lion and the bear? David, is it thou, the youth who of all the sons of Jesse was chosen by Samuel to be the king of Israel? David, is it thou, the youth who with his sling and his trust in God slew the blasphemous Goliath? David, is it thou, who with thy harp didst drive out the evil spirit from gloomy Saul? David, is it thou whom Jonathan loved so tenderly? David, is it thou who when Saul, thine enemy, was in thy hand, didst twice spare him, refusing to smite the Lord's anointed? David, is it thou, the singer of the Psalms which still breathe and express in deepest melody the noblest aspirations, the grandest faith and trust, the deepest sorrows of the Christian? Yes, David, alas, it is thou! Would that thou hadst fallen first on the field of battle. Holy angels, who are wont to frequent this sacred house, withdraw now for a little, we pray thee, from this place! Holy angels, withdraw; for if too sad this spectacle for man to behold, what, holy angels, unfallen spirits of God, must it be to you. Withdraw! Withdraw and leave us to mourn alone over this adulterer and murderer who once was the man after God's own heart.

But all these things are written for our admonition, and we are glad that the Holy Spirit who inspired this record, and inspired the songs and prayers of David, did not spare us the story of his fall, for even in his fall David is our friend and our teacher. Here we learn how sin, even the worst of sins, attacks the godly man. No past devotion, no past confession, no past prayers, not yesterday's resolve and repentance, but only the repentance and the faith and the prayers of today can keep us out of temptation and deliver us from sin.

PETER AND THE SADNESS OF SIN AS A DISCIPLE OF CHRIST

It is midnight on the night of nights. The fire burns in the courtyard of the high priests. Servants, soldiers, hangers on, and two disciples are standing about that fire. A door opens into a chamber off the courtyard and Jesus is led out, bleeding from the cruel blows which have been showered upon Him, mocked, insulted, and spat upon. Just at that moment a loud, angry voice rings out through the courtyard, saying with coarse oaths, "I never knew him!"

Who can this be? Is it the man whom his brother Andrew brought to Christ, and looking upon whom Jesus said, "Thy name is Simon. Henceforth it shall be Peter, the Rock"? Is it the man who fell at the feet of Christ in the fishing boat and sounded the prayer for all penitents, "Depart from me, O God, for I am a sinful man"? Is it the man who when Christ asked his disciples to tell Him who he was, confessed, "Thou art the Christ, the Son of the living God"? Is it the man who, when many of his disciples forsook Him, answered the plaintive question of Jesus, "Will ye also leave me and go away?" with that great word which still in every crisis in life keeps the follower of Christ from the abyss of unbelief, "Lord, to whom shall we go? Thou hast the words of Eternal Life"? Is it the man whom Christ took up to the Mount of Transfiguration, and who was so inspired by what he saw and heard that he wanted to build three tabernacles and stay there forever? Is it the man who said though all others forsook Christ he would not leave him?

Is it the man who with splendid courage drew his sword, and undaunted faced the mob in the garden of Gethsemane?

Yes, Peter, alas, it is thou! Thou art the man! All of heaven's sorrow and amazement is in that look of Christ when He looked upon Peter that night, and the saddest tears that were ever wept were the tears of Peter when he went out that night and wept bitterly.

These men show in their life's history the sadness of sin and prove, what really needs no proof, that sin is the saddest word in the Bible and in human speech. But the Bible is the perfect and eternal mirror of the human heart. Do not imagine that this is just past history, or just Biblical history. No, read the papers, read the best sellers, read the story of the lives of men and women about you, read your own life, and you will see that the sin of Cain, man's inhumanity to man, still makes the earth a sad place; that gifted and noble men like Saul are wrecked and ruined by sin, that godly men like David can be brought low in the dust, even by the sins of the flesh, and that men and women who follow Christ, and in their hearts love Him, can yet strangely and sadly deny Him.

But there is one more life which reveals the supreme sadness of sin. Three crosses on a lonely, barren, skull-shaped hill, a thief on this cross and a murderer on that; and between them a man with a crown of thorns on his head and blood flowing from his hands and his feet and his side, while those in front of His cross jeer at Him and mock Him. And who is this? This is the Son of Man, the Son of God, the One altogether lovely, the Prince of Peace. This is He before Whom seraphim and cherubim fall down and veil their faces. And yet He hangs bleeding, reviled, and forsaken on a cursed tree! What brought Him there? What did this terrible deed? What made Immanuel cry out, "Behold and see if there be any sorrow like unto my sorrow"? It was sin! Your sin and my sin nailed Him to the Cross. There we behold the deepest and darkest sadness of sin. No wonder the sun could not endure it and veiled His face; no wonder the stable earth shook to its foundations.

But wait! Sin has overreached itself on the Cross. The blow that it struck when it crucified Christ came the blow of liberation for all the victims of sin. Sin's masterpiece of sadness became God's masterpiece of forgiveness and mercy. Through that death sin itself, for the believer in Christ, is crucified. That death is the foundation of our hope, the prediction of our triumph.

Thus the saddest word and the saddest theme become the gladdest word and the most joyful theme. The world has enough sadness in it caused by sin. See that you do not add to that sadness. Has anyone here tonight been hurt by sin, saddened by sin, your own sin or the sin of another? Then come to the Cross. Here fervently kneel. Here is the remedy. Earth hath no sorrow that heaven cannot heal.

2

THE MOST BEAUTIFUL WORD

What is the most beautiful word, in the Bible or out of it, spoken in heaven, or upon earth? Some thought that mother is the most beautiful word. And a tender and beautiful word it is. Some thought that grace is the most beautiful word.

> Grace! 'tis a charming sound,
> Harmonious to mine ear.
> Heaven with the echo shall resound
> And all the earth shall bear.
> —Rev. Philip Doddridge

Some thought that salvation is the most beautiful word. "They shall call thy gates praise and thy walls salvation." Some thought that Jesus is the most beautiful word.

> How sweet the name of Jesus sounds
> In a believer's ear.
> It soothes his sorrows, heals his wounds,
> And drives away his tear.
> —Rev. John Newton

Some voted that come is the most beautiful word in the Bible. It is, indeed, one of the great words of the Bible. "Come, now, let us reason together, saith the Lord." "Come, for all things are ready." "Come unto me and I will give you rest."

17

The Bible comes to a close with the sweet music of that come. "The Spirit and the bride say, come. And let him that heareth say, come. And let him that is athirst, come. And whosoever will, let him take the water of life freely."

But by far the greater number said that love is the most beautiful word in the Bible and in human speech. "Now abideth these three—faith, hope, and love, and the greatest of these is love." But the most beautiful word in the Bible, the most beautiful word spoken in heaven or on earth, is the word *forgiveness*. There you have love in action, for "herein is love, not that we loved God, but that God loved us and gave His Son to be a propitiation for our sins." Like all the colors of the rainbow, this word forgiveness includes all the attributes of God: His wisdom, power, holiness, justice, goodness, and truth. "There is forgiveness with Thee"—Psalm 130:4.

Sin is the saddest word in the Bible and in human speech, but forgiveness is the most beautiful word because it cancels the effects of sin. It takes away the sorrow and the darkness of sin, as the light of the sun scatters the darkness of the night. "Where sin abounded, grace—and that is only another word for forgiveness—did much more abound."

Forgiveness is the most beautiful word because it kindles the most beautiful light in the face of God or in the countenance of man. It is the most beautiful word because it is the costliest word. Before God could pronounce it, Christ had to die on the Cross. It is the word that the Apostles and the angels like to pronounce. It is the word that is dearest to every true believer. It is the word that will awaken the music of the redeemed in heaven, for that is what they sing about there, the forgiveness of God—"Now unto Him that loved us and hath washed us from our sins by His own blood."

As in the case of sin, the saddest of all words, I shall try to prove that forgiveness is the most beautiful of all words, not by abstract reasoning, but by illustration in the lives of men and women in the Bible.

JOSEPH AND THE FORGIVENESS OF HIS BRETHREN

Pronounce the name of Joseph, and almost every chord in human nature and in human experience commences to vibrate.

One morning he appeared at the encampment of his brethren on the plains of Dothan, his coat of many colors adorned with flashing jewels, the drops of dew which he had swept from the flowers as he passed. His jealous, envious brothers saw him afar off, for hate can see a long distance, and said, "Behold this dreamer cometh. Come let us slay him, and we will see what will come of his dreams." One day they were to see.

Never was a more heartless or more cruel crime committed than that which his brothers committed against Joseph. His lot was slavery in Egypt, and then worse than slavery, the false charge of a wicked woman whose temptations he had repulsed. Then the long years in prison, forgotten by those whom he had befriended. But one day, when all these troubles were over and Joseph had the second place in Pharaoh's Kingdom, the bite of famine brought the sons of Jacob down into Egypt to buy corn. They did not know Joseph, but Joseph remembered them at once and spoke roughly with them and charged them with being spies, and asked pointed questions about the number of brothers they had, and about their youngest brother. Then he kept Simeon as a hostage and required them, if they came back, to bring their youngest brother with them. To this, with breaking heart, the aged Jacob reluctantly consented. And once again the brothers went down to Egypt. This time, when they started homeward, Joseph's silver cup was found in Benjamin's sack, and they were brought trembling with fear once more into the presence of Joseph, who said that the man in whose sack his cup had been found should remain in Egypt as his slave, but the rest could go home.

Then Judah made one of the most beautiful speeches of the Bible, and when he had concluded, Joseph, no longer able to refrain himself, wept aloud and made himself known to his brothers. "Come near to me, I pray you. I am Joseph, your brother, whom ye sold into Egypt. Now, therefore, be not grieved nor angry with yourselves that ye sold me hither, for God did send me before you to preserve life."

Thus Joseph forgave his brothers. Seventeen years later, when Jacob was dead, Joseph's brothers feared that now he would take vengeance upon them for the crime they had committed against him. Guilt always fears, and finds it difficult to believe in human forgiveness. But when they came to him with what probably was a forged message from Jacob, saying that when he was dying he asked that Joseph should forgive his brethren, Joseph said, "Fear not, am I in the place of God? As for you, ye thought evil against me, but God meant it unto good." Thus, Joseph forgave his brothers and comforted them. That is why Joseph is the most Christian man in the Old Testament. The most bitter feuds, the most devastating hatreds, alas, are those which smolder and burn in family relationships. There, most of all, it is hardest to forgive. But Joseph forgave his brethren. Before Christ preached the Sermon on the Mount, Joseph practiced it. Before Paul taught that all things work together for good, Joseph, by forgiving his brothers, showed that he ordered his life on that principle.

CHRIST AND THE WOMAN WHO WAS A SINNER

Perhaps the four most beautiful scenes in the New Testament are scenes of forgiveness; the return and forgiveness of the Prodigal Son, the repentance and the forgiveness of Peter, the repentance and forgiveness of the dying thief, and the forgiveness of the woman who was a sinner.

Simon the Pharisee had invited Jesus to dine with him. We wonder why he did this. Was it out of curiosity? Or was it because Jesus was now becoming a notable person, and notable persons will always get invitations from those who like to shine in their light? Whatever the motive, Jesus, who ate with publicans and sinners, accepted the invitation of this wealthy and distinguished Pharisee. But at the feast Simon disclosed his true nature. He omitted the ordinary courtesies of the East—the kiss of salutation, oil for the head, and water for the feet. Perhaps he thought that since Jesus was just a carpenter's son the usual social amenities could be omitted. Or, it may be, and that is more likely, that he went out of the way to humiliate Jesus. It was said of Walter Scott that he treated all men as if they were blood relations. Not even the humblest man ever felt abashed in the presence of Abraham Lincoln. But Simon tries to humiliate Jesus.

As the feast proceeded, the woman who was a sinner made her entry, bringing with her an alabaster box of ointment, costly and precious, purchased, no doubt, with past wages of sin. We wonder where she had heard of Christ. Perhaps she had stood on the fringe of a crowd one day and had heard His words, "Come unto me and I will give you rest." It may have been just the tone of His voice, or the light on his Face. Thomas Arnold used to say, and what is very encouraging for a minister, that no church service is ever held without some one person being impressed. Who knows but one day when Jesus was speaking it was the woman who was a sinner whom he reached, and the only one?

Rossetti's painting and poem describe the woman going up the steps of Simon's house followed by her lover who seeks to hold her back. But now she has found the true Lover; she has seen her Bridegroom's face and must go in.

> O loose me! Seest thou not my Bridegroom's face,
> That draws me to Him? For His feet my kiss,
> My hair, my eyes, He craves today:—And oh!
> What words can tell what other day and place
> Shall see me clasp those blood-stained feet of His?
> He needs me, calls me, loves me; let me go!

It was easy for her to approach Jesus as He reclined at Simon's table. First she poured the precious ointment on His head, then with her tears she washed His feet and dried them with the golden hair of her head. Once she had used that hair as a net to entice her victims. Now she used it to wipe the feet of her new found Lover, the Son of Man. What a sight for men and for angels! We are glad that that head that was soon to be crowned with thorns was anointed with the precious ointment that night, and that those feet, soon to be pierced with nails, were washed with the tears of contrition and of affection.

At the end of this beautiful scene, after he had rebuked Simon for his unspoken criticism, Jesus said, "Her sins, which are many, are forgiven, for she loveth much." And to her He said, "Thy sins are forgiven." How true that is! The more we feel our need of Christ, the greater our sense of forgiveness, and the deeper our love for Christ.

As this forgiven woman goes out from the banqueting hall, I hear strains of haunting melody. Whence comes this music? It is not the orchestra of Simon, nor that of strolling musicians, nor music coming from some house where there is marriage or revelry. It seems to come down out of the skies. Are the morning stars singing together again, and are all the sons of God shouting for joy? No; it is not the music, but something richer, deeper, more majestic. It is the music in which all the minor chords of human guilt or shame or sorrow and suffering and pain, touched by the sighs and the agony and tears and the blood of Christ, have been awakened into the major chord of thanksgiving and rejoicing. It is heaven's holiest music, the song of the angels rejoicing over one sinner that repenteth.

PETER'S MORNING

We parted with Peter at the saddest hour of his life, when, after his denial of Christ, he "went out and wept bitterly." Now we meet him again at the morning, in the most beautiful hour of his life, when, on that memorable morning on the Sea of Galilee, Peter, holding on to the bulging nets, heard John's ejaculation, "It is the Lord!" and wrapping his fisherman's cloak around him, for he was naked, plunged into the sea to get to that Lord. During the meal which followed I imagine that there was much silence. Indeed, John in his account says that they durst not ask Him anything. They must have been wondering, and perhaps Peter, too, what Christ would say to Peter. If so, they were not kept long in suspense, for when the meal was over Jesus turned to Peter and said—What? Not, "How could you ever have done it, Peter?" "How do you dare to be found among my disciples after that cruel denial?" "What is the difference between your sin and that of Judas?" Not that, but this, "Peter, lovest thou me?" And when Peter had thrice confessed his love for Christ, Christ said to him, "Peter, feed my sheep." That was Peter's beautiful morning when he heard the word of forgiveness on the lips of his risen Lord. The sea and the Galilean hills were all glorious that morning with the light of the risen sun, but there was a brighter glory, a light never seen on land or sea in the face of Jesus and in the face of Peter that morning. It was the light of forgiveness.

THE DYING THIEF

The saddest hour earth ever saw was that hour when Christ hung disowned, dishonored, and forsaken between two thieves. There sin struck its most fearful blow and pronounced its most fearful word. But that was not all! There was another word that was spoken. The dying thief turned to Jesus, and with repentance on his heart and on his lips, said, "Jesus, remember me when Thou comest in Thy Kingdom!" Then from the lips of the dying Savior came those words of forgiveness, "Today shalt thou be with me in Paradise." Him, first of all, that penitent thief and murderer, Jesus took into Paradise, and all the angels and all the archangels, and all the seraphim and all the cherubim came out of the gates of heaven to greet a forgiven thief.

Yes, there is no doubt about it. Forgiveness is the most beautiful of all words. But are you able to pronounce it? Can you freely from the heart forgive one another, even as God for Christ's sake hath forgiven you? If not, remember those words of Jesus, "If ye forgive not men their trespasses, neither will your Heavenly Father forgive you your trespasses." Give no sleep to the eyes, nor slumber to the eyelids, until you can pronounce this most beautiful of all words.

Have you heard this word yourself on the lips of Christ spoken to you? The woman who was a sinner heard it; the publican who went up to the temple to pray heard it; Peter, who denied Him, heard it; the thief on the cross heard it; the man born blind heard it; the Apostle Paul heard it. You, too, can hear it, the most beautiful of all words, the light of earth, the glory of heaven—"Thy sins are forgiven."

3

THE WORD THAT NEVER COMES BACK

What is the word that never comes back? Some thought it was depart, some voted for yesterday, and some for today. Others thought it was opportunity, and others voted for time, and others for death. Many of these were not far from the right word.

What is the word? What is the word that never comes back, even if the world were to run on for a thousand million years? What is the word that is able to work miracles? The word by which kingdoms have been conquered, destinies achieved, the gates of heaven opened, and eternal life won or lost? The word is *now*—2 Corinthians 6:2. Now never comes back. It is the one precious, invaluable portion of time that belongs to you and me because it is the only portion of time about which we can be sure and in which we know we can act.

> The clock of life is wound but once,
> And no man has the power
> To tell just when the hands will stop,
> At late or early hour.
>
> —Rev. B. Meyer

As in the case of the saddest word and the most beautiful word, when we come to the word that never comes back we shall demonstrate that now is that word, not by generalizations or abstract reasoning, but by illustrations from the lives of men in the Bible. Thus we shall see what now, made use of or sinned against and neglected, meant to men and women in the Bible and what it means to men and women today.

ESAU

Esau, "that profane person," illustrates in the story of his life how spiritual powers and graces neglected, sinned against, or despised now, today, may be forfeited and lost forever.

Esau is handed down from generation to generation in the words of the Letter to the Hebrews as "that profane person who for one morsel of pottage sold his birthright." This was how it happened: Esau was a cunning hunter, a man of the field; whereas his brother Jacob was a plain man dwelling in tents. One day Esau came in from the fields faint with hunger. As he drew near to the encampment the odor of the savory pottage that Jacob was cooking smote his nostrils. Esau said to Jacob, "Feed me, I pray thee, with that same red pottage, for I am faint." The shrewd and crafty Jacob, taking advantage of the intense hunger of Esau, saw an opportunity to get from him the privileged birthright, so he made to Esau the ignominious proposal that he would give him the pottage in exchange for the birthright. Just at that moment Esau was thinking only of satisfying his appetite. The birthright could not be eaten; the pottage could, and there it was, steaming in Jacob's pot. Esau exclaimed, "Behold, I am at the point to die, and what profit shall this birthright be to me?" In effect, he said, "Take the birthright if you want it. What I want, and what I want now, is that mess of pottage." So the bargain was struck. In the ancient record this is the story of it: "Then Jacob gave Esau bread and pottage of lentils, and he did eat and drink and rose up and went his way. Thus Esau despised his birthright."

One hardly knows which of these two men to despise more at this moment—Jacob who capitalized the hunger of his brother, or Esau who sold the birthright for the mess of pottage. Some years afterwards, by another shrewd act, and this time a crafty deception in which his mother assisted him, Jacob passed himself off for Esau before the dimming eyes of the dying Isaac and got the blessing that belonged to the first-born. When Esau came in from the field and found out what had happened, he cried with a great and "exceeding bitter cry" and said unto his father, "Bless me, even me also, O my father!" And Esau lifted up his voice and wept!

There you have the other Esau, the Esau who has regard for something else than pottage, and who wants his father's blessing, and who would like to have back the birthright which he had so basely and cheaply sold to his brother. It was the infamous deceit of Jacob that had brought Esau to his present pitiable condition. Yet the reference to the incident in the twelfth chapter of the Letter to the Hebrews makes the calamity which had befallen Esau, that is, the loss of the blessing of the first-born, the direct result and the divine retribution for his conduct when he had estimated his birthright as of less value than a mess of pottage, for there it is written, "The profane person who for one morsel of meat sold his birthright; for ye know now that afterward when he would have inherited the blessing he was rejected, for he found no place of repentance though he sought it carefully with tears."

That is a striking and a solemn record. No change of mind now, no change of heart on the part of Esau could get him back what he had basely forfeited. Once he sold his birthright for pottage; now he weeps bitter tears at the thought of the loss of the blessing that went with it. But that could not undo what in a moment of physical appetite he had done. He had sinned against his spiritual nature in that all-important moment that we call now, and when another day came, and with it another mood, no tears, no searching, no regret, could get back what he had forfeited and lost. How many, alas, live to echo Esau's bitter cry! Inflamed with some desire or passion, they despised and trampled on some spiritual gift or power. Then one day they awoke with bitter regret and remorse to the knowledge of what they had lost. Esau afterwards became a useful man, and with noble magnanimity long years afterwards forgave his brother Jacob his heinous transgression and sin. But he never got back what he had thrown away to satisfy the desire and appetite of a moment.

> Break, break, break, on thy gray crags, O sea,
> But the vanished grace of a day that is gone
> Will never come back to me.
>
> —Tennyson

Now! How solemn and beautiful is that Now! Do not sin against your now, so that tomorrow you will mourn over its irrevocable loss.

THE PARABLE OF THE LOST PRISONER

Here we have set forth how now is the time for conquering temptation and destroying an evil habit.

This is one of the great parables of the Old Testament. Israel had won a battle over her inveterate enemy Ben-hadad, the King of Syria. Because of a previous defeat in the hill country, the vanquished Syrians concluded that the Hebrew God was a God of the hills, and that if they could have a battle in the plains it would have a different issue than the battle in the hills. But the battle in the plains proved even more disastrous than the battle on the hills. A hundred thousand Syrians fell in the combat and twenty thousand perished in the earthquake at the end of the battle. The army of Syria had been destroyed, but the heart and soul of the army, the crafty Ben-hadad, still lived. From his hiding place Ben-hadad sent messengers to the King of Israel, Ahab. Elated over his easy victory, Ahab, instead of destroying Ben-hadad, or at least taking such measures as would have prevented further hostilities on his part, invited him to ride with him in his chariot and sent him off to Syria with easy terms of peace which Ben-hadad at once proceeded to violate.

Then God sent one of the Sons of the Prophets to condemn Ahab for his folly and announce his judgment. This Son of the Prophets had one of his companions smite him on the head and wound him. Then, in the disguise of a wounded soldier and with a bandage around his head, he sat lamenting by the roadside. Presently the chariot of Ahab came rolling by from the field of battle, when the Son of the Prophets sprang up, and addressing the king, said, "Thy servant went out into the midst of the battle, and behold a man turned aside and brought a man unto me and said, 'Keep this man. If by any means he be missing, then shall thy life be for his life, or else thou shall pay a talent of silver.' And as thy servant was busy here and there, he was gone."

The purpose of the parable, of course, was to get Ahab to pronounce judgment upon himself, and this Ahab quickly did. He said to the supposed soldier, "So shall thy judgment be. Thyself hast decided it." Then the prophet unwound the bandage about his head and said, "Because thou hast let go out of thy hand a man whom I appointed to utter destruction, therefore thy life shall go for his life and thy people for his people." Three years afterwards, Ahab and Jehoshaphat, the King of Judah, were going into battle against this same Ben-hadad at Ramoth-Gilead. Remembering the words of this nameless prophet spoken three years before, at the close of that other battle, Ahab was alarmed, and put aside his royal robes and disguised himself as a common soldier. "But a certain man drew a bow at a venture," and Ahab was slain.

Ahab was slain and Israel beaten in battle by the very king who once was in the power of Ahab, either to bind him or to destroy him. But in his folly he let him go, and the king who was thus spared conquered and slew Ahab.

There are times when we are stirred and aroused as to some un-Christlike trait or some passion or evil habit in our life. We see the unloveliness of it, the sin of it, the future menace that it holds over our life. Then we have it in our power to conquer it and destroy it. The time to kill any evil thing in your life, to break the chains of any evil habit, is never tomorrow, but always today, never then, but always now. A gentleman who used to come to our Tuesday Noon Meeting told me at the close of one of our meetings of a turning point in his life. As a young railroad man he had been going with his fellow employees frequently to a saloon. Then one day the thought came to him, "I'd better stop this; I'd better break this habit, and the time to do it is now." He did stop it. He did break the habit, and now an old man, he told me he had never again gone into a saloon. He made use of that all-important and all-precious portion of time that we call now. Now is the time!

CHRIST AND THE SLEEPING DISCIPLES

Here we have the now for the ministry of friendship and affection, a now which never comes back. It was one of the saddest and darkest and most critical hours in the life of our Lord. He left the eight disciples near the gates of the Garden of Gethsemane, and taking with him Peter and James and John went a little farther into the recesses of the garden. Then removing even from these three he went a stone's throw farther, and there falling on his knees entered into his agony. But before leaving Peter and James and John he asked them to watch while he went yonder to pray. Twice he came back from his agony and prayer, when his sweat was as it were great drops of blood falling to the ground, and found the disciples sleeping, and twice He exclaimed in sad amazement as He awakened them, "What, could ye not watch with me one hour!" But when He came back the third time and found them again asleep, and once more awakened them, what was it that he said? What were those memorable words that the angels overheard as they hovered near that battleground of Christ? They were these, "Sleep on, now, and take your rest, for the Son of Man is betrayed into the hands of sinners."

Peter and James and John were all to write a noble history and make a noble witness to that Lord during whose agony and bloody sweat they had so ignobly slumbered. At least two of them were to seal their fate with martyr's blood. But there was one thing that they never had a chance to do again, and that was to watch with Jesus in the hour of His agony and sore battle as He knelt over the cup of the world's iniquity and sin.

Now is the time for your ministry to those whom you love. How true those pathetic words with which Jesus rebuked the disciples when they criticized Mary's costly gift of ointment, and said it might better have been sold and the money given to the poor. "The poor ye have always with ye, but Me ye have not always." The generality of people, and souls who need help and encouragement and comfort, them you have always with you, always about you. But there are others and near to you, whom you have not always with you. The only time for ministry to them is now, today. Never then, never tomorrow.

> O such a little while, alas, have we
> To gentle be and kind.
>
> —Author Unknown

These are homely lines and yet bring out effectively the importance of now when it comes to this matter of ministry to your friends.

> If with pleasure you are viewing
> Any work a man is doing;
> 　If you like him or you love him, tell him now.
> Don't withhold your approbation
> Till the parson makes oration
> 　And he lies with snowy lilies o'er his brow.

> For no matter how you shout it,
> He won't really care about it;
> 　He won't know how many tear-drops you have shed.
> If you think some praise is due him,
> Now's the time to slip it to him,
> 　For he cannot read his tombstone when he's dead.

> More than fame and more than money
> Is a comment kind and sunny,
> 　And the hearty, warm approval of a friend;
> For it gives to life a savor,
> And it makes you stronger, braver,
> 　And it gives you heart and spirit to the end.

> If he earns your praise, bestow it,
> If you like him, let him know it.
> 　Let the words of true encouragement be said;
> Do not wait till life is over,
> And he's underneath the clover,
> 　For be cannot read his tombstone when he's dead.
>
> —Author Unknown

THE BRIDEGROOM AND THE DOOR THAT WAS SHUT

Here we have the now that is the greatest and most important of all, the now for repentance and faith and the Kingdom of God. This is a part of what seems to have been the last public sermon of our Lord spoken to His disciples on the Mount of Olives. The Ten Virgins had set out with their lamps or torches to greet the Bridegroom. Five of them had taken oil in their vessels with their lamps ready for any delay or emergency, but five took no oil with them. There was a long delay. The Bridegroom tarried, and while he tarried they all slumbered and slept. Then at midnight there was the cry, "Behold, the Bridegroom cometh! Go ye out to meet Him!" Then the Ten Virgins hastened to light their lamps, but the lamps of the five who had brought no oil with them sputtered and flickered for a little and soon went out. Unable to borrow from their sisters, they hurried off to get oil from those who bought and sold, and while they were doing this the Bridegroom came, and they that were ready went in with Him to the marriage, "and the door was shut." Shortly afterwards the other five came hurrying to the Bridegroom's mansion and knocked excitedly on the door, and cried, "Lord, open to us!" But the Bridegroom from within answered, "Verily, I say unto you, I know ye not."

And the door was shut! No words in the Bible are more solemn than that. And it was the Lord of mercy and compassion and tears Himself who uttered them! Once the door was open! Now it was closed. O golden door of repentance! How many have passed over thy portals and with rejoicing have greeted the Bridegroom and entered into Eternal Life. For everyone of us tonight the door is open, and over that door I see written in letters of gold, traced there by the pierced hand of Immanuel Himself, *now*. Will you enter that door? Now is the acceptable time. Now is the day of salvation.

I saw a heavenly spirit standing and weeping by the portals of my church, and I said to him, "Heavenly Spirit, Heavenly Visitor, why standest thou here, and why weepest thou?" And the heavenly visitor answered, "I stand here and weep over those to whose souls I once spoke through the message of this church, and for whom the door was opened, and tonight it is shut. Now is the acceptable time!

4

THE HARDEST WORD

What is the hardest word, in the Bible or out of it? What is the word that is the most difficult of all words to pronounce? Some thought that word was duty, and duty is indeed a hard word. Some thought that it was repent, and man does find it very hard to repent. Others surmised that it was hate, and others hell, and still others death. Some voted that yes is the hardest of all words. One boy put down stone!

But none of these is the hardest word. What is that word, one of the shortest, and yet one with the longest echo of all words? What is the word, the lack of which set the world on the wrong track from the beginning? What is the word by pronouncing which prophets and apostles became great? What is this word which lays a foundation upon which to build character? What is the word by the power of which kingdoms and empires have been won, and for the lack of which they have been lost? What is the word which has secured happiness and a bright destiny for men, and the lack of which has condemned them unto failure, penury, and woe? What is the word that in the great crisis of his life Jesus Christ pronounced and thereby conquered Satan and became our Redeemer? That word, the hardest in the Bible or out of it, the hardest in English, French, German, Spanish, Arabic, Greek, Hebrew, Egyptian, is the short but mighty word *no*. That was what the three Hebrew lads said to Nebuchadnezzar when he commanded them to bow down to his golden image and threatened them with the fiery furnace if they did not. They answered, "No! We will not"—Daniel 3:18.

Some time ago the editor of one of our magazines which specializes in word study asked a small number of distinguished writers to answer the following questions:

1. What word to you in English seems the most beautiful in sound?

2. What English word seems to you the most useful in the language?

3. What word to you seems the most annoyingly used or misused?

In answer to the first question, the most beautiful word, some of the old favorites were given. Among them the musical word Mesopotamia. This is the word the great English actor Garrick wished he could pronounce the way the famous preacher George Whitefield pronounced it. Nearly all agreed that the most misused word was yes, and nearly all voted that the most useful word in the language is no.

Plutarch tells of an ancient town whose inhabitants became slaves and vassals to others because of their inability to say no. The inability, or unwillingness, to say no has made men slaves to others, and still worse, slaves to their passions and their fears. For the lack of a no spoken to the tempter, man fell in the beginning, and the world started on the wrong track. Adam was a great lexicographer, the master of vocabulary, for we are told that he was able to give names to all the birds of the air and the beasts of the field, but he was not able to pronounce the most useful and the most difficult word in human speech, no. That early beginning is the true picture of human life from age to age. Almost as soon as we cross the threshold of life we are assailed by enemies, and if we lack the power to say no we are doomed. One of General Grant's most useful generals, the one who had the greatest influence on Grant's conduct, was his able and faithful chief-of-staff, General John Rawlins. Grant says of him that he knew how to say no to a request which he felt ought not to be granted, and say it in such a way that the man who made the request never repeated it.

As in the case of the other words, so with this word no; we shall prove and demonstrate that it is the hardest word, but also one of the greatest, by illustration in the lives of men and women in the Bible.

JOSEPH AND NO TO THE TEMPTATIONS OF THE FLESH

Joseph was an illustration of the most beautiful word forgiveness, but he is also an illustration of the hardest word, no. After the temptation of Jesus Himself, the temptation of Joseph is the most celebrated story of temptation, and the most useful, especially to young men.

Sold by his brothers into Egypt, Joseph was bought as a slave by Potiphar, the captain of Pharaoh's guard. In Potiphar's house, the splendid qualities of Joseph soon lifted him to a position of honor and trust. Then Potiphar's wife fell in love with Joseph and tempted him to dishonor and sin. The more one reads that story the more one wonders that Joseph was able to pronounce that magnificent no. He was then in his early twenties and in the full tide of his natural life. The most natural of temptations, that of the body, is also the strongest and the most dangerous.

This temptation was unusually strong because of the person of the tempter. She was not a common woman or a streetwalker, but a woman of rank and beauty and fashion. From a standpoint of worldly policy, as well as from the urge of natural appetite, this temptation, if yielded to, seemed to promise advancement for Joseph. He would have been an influential friend at court. But to refuse would be to render himself the victim of hatred and anger and jeopardize his very life. It was a strong temptation because it was a repeated temptation. Some men will say no once or twice, and then surrender. This woman tempted Joseph day after day. Constantly he was in the presence of temptation, and yet day after day he repulsed it. It was a strong temptation, too, because the man who was tempted was a youth who was a slave and an exile in a foreign land. His father's people and his father's religion, apparently, had done little for him. Slaves were not supposed to have virtue. No doubt the thought came to Joseph, "Why bother about these old Hebrew scruples? It will be both for my advantage and my pleasure to yield."

Yet Joseph met the temptation with a magnificent no. The

consideration which held him true to himself and true to virtue and to honor was the thought of God. "How," he cried, "can I do this great evil and sin against God?" An old drama represents Potiphar's wife, when Joseph said that, as throwing her skirt over the head of a god which stood in the chamber, and saying, "Now God cannot see." But Joseph answered, "My God sees. How can I do this great evil and sin against God?"

The angry, infuriated woman made a false charge against Joseph, and Joseph was cast into prison. It looked as if Joseph had lost everything, but in reality he had won everything, and that no was the turning point in Joseph's career. His path took him now through a rough, dark dungeon, but it emerged at length in the sunlight of national splendor and honor. It is always so. When a man yields to this kind of temptation, then farewell to the tranquil mind, farewell to true greatness. But where the temptation is resisted, where the tempted says to the tempter, "No, I will not," immediately invisible hands begin to forge a chain of gold which one day will be hung about the victor's neck. The greatest weapon for the days of youth is a no, which is founded upon the fear of God.

> When ranting round in pleasure's ring,
> Religion may be blinded;
> Or if she gie a random sting,
> It may be little minded;
> But when in life we're tempest-driven
> A conscience but a canker—
> A correspondence fix'd wi' Heaven,
> Is sure a noble anchor!
>
> —Robert Burns

THE HEBREW LAD'S AND NEBUCHADNEZZAR'S IMAGE

Here we have the no of religious principle and conviction. Shadrach, Meshach, and Abednego, the Chaldean names which had been given to the three companions of Daniel who were being brought up with him at the court of Nebuchadnezzar, had refused to worship the golden image that Nebuchadnezzar had set up. Heralds had gone throughout the land shouting to the people, "To you it is commanded, O people, nations and languages, that at what time ye hear the sound of the cornet, flute, harp, sackbut, psaltery, dulcimer, and all kinds of music, ye fall down and worship the golden image that Nebuchadnezzar the king hath set up. And whoso falleth not down and worshippeth shall at the same hour be cast into the midst of a burning fiery furnace."

The Hebrew lads had been brought up on the Second Commandment, "Thou shalt not make unto thee any graven image. Thou shalt not bow down thyself to them nor serve them." Therefore they refused to prostrate themselves before this golden image of the king on the plains of Dura. Their enemies among the Chaldeans were glad of an opportunity to accuse the Hebrews to the King. When Nebuchadnezzar heard that they had refused to bow down, in his rage and fury he had his officers bring them into his presence. He said to them, "Is it true, O Shadrach, Meshach, Abednego, do not serve my gods nor worship the golden image which I have set up? If ye will not worship, ye shall be cast the same hour into the midst of a burning, fiery furnace; and who is that God that shall deliver you out of my hands?"

Then the three Hebrew youths made their grand answer, rendered their magnificent no that still echoes in heaven and on earth: "O Nebuchadnezzar, our God whom we serve is able to deliver us from the fiery furnace, and he will deliver us out of thy hand, O King. But if not, be it known unto thee, O King, that we will not serve thy gods, nor worship the golden image which thou hast set up."

The grand thing about their answer was the word, "But if not." They knew that God was able to deliver them. But whether it pleased Him to deliver them or not, their duty was clear, and they chose to burn to ashes in the fiery furnace rather than bow down to a heathen god. On this occasion God did deliver them. After they had been cast into the furnace the flames of which were so hot that they consumed the men who threw them into it, Nebuchadnezzar went down to contemplate their fate. Perhaps he wondered if the God of Israel had been able to deliver them. When he looked in he saw the three Hebrew lads, and by their side the Form of a Fourth, and the

Form of the Fourth was like the Son of God. The smell of fire had not passed on them. God had rewarded their fidelity with a great deliverance.

> The Three, when Jesus made the Fourth,
> Found fire as soft as air.
>
> —Author Unknown

Even if they had not been delivered, even if their bodies had been burned to ashes, still it would be a great story, a magnificent stand for principle and for faith. When someone told Athanasius, the great defender of the Trinitarian faith, that the whole world was against him, he simply replied, "Then I am against the world."

Vashti and a Woman's No

This is another great no that comes ringing down to us out of the Old Testament. For seven days a great banquet had been staged by Ahasuerus in his capital at Shushan. One hundred and twenty-seven of the princes of the provinces were assembled from all parts of the world. The scene was one of Oriental splendor and magnificence. The cups out of which the princes and the lords drank were of pure gold and each one was chased with a different design. The couches upon which the banqueters sat or reclined were of silver and gold, and decorated with the beasts and deities of Persian superstition. The floor was of red, blue, and white marble. Beautiful marble columns sustained the roof of the banqueting house, under which was hung the great veil or canopy of white, green, and blue velvet, caught with streamers of fine linen and purple to silver rings sunk in the columns. This was the stage and setting for one of history's most splendid refusals.

When all the lords and nobles and revellers were well drunken, the maudlin Ahasuerus, thinking to startle and entertain his guests, resolved on something that was unheard of heretofore, even at a Persian banquet. They had plenty of women, dancing girls from the Caucasus and Damascus, but it was something more than this that Ahasuerus had in mind. He would expose the Queen, Vashti, and exhibit her charms to this drunken crew. So he sent for his chamberlains and gave them the brutal order, "Bring in Vashti, the Queen! The beauty of the whole earth." The seven chamberlains looked into each other's faces in frightened amazement for a moment and then hurried off to the harem to summon Vashti. The lords and nobles, roused out of their drunken stupor by the unprecedented proposal, lifted themselves to a sitting posture and eagerly looked towards the vast door, curtained by the white, green, and blue portieres.

At length the heavy curtains are pushed back and Mehuman, the chief of the chamberlains, with a frightened look on his countenance, advances to the royal seat and whispers to the king, "The Queen will not come in." Enraged and drunken though he is, Vashti knows that he dare not compel her. "But the Queen Ahasuerus refused to come at the King's command." Vashti had counted the cost. She knew what it meant—disgrace, dethronement, banishment, perhaps death, by poisoned cup or shining steel. But she is willing to pay the cost. She will not strip her veil of modesty by exposing herself to the lewd glances and lascivious gestures of the drunken crew who sit at the table of Ahasuerus. Vashti utters her magnificent no, teaches her deathless lesson, and disappears from the stage to make room for that other woman, the Hebrew maid, Esther, in whose greater renown her own splendid witness is too often forgotten.

The palace of Shushan and the proud city of Ahasuerus today are only a heap of dust where wild beasts howl. But searching amid this heap of dust we come upon this flaming jewel of Vashti's noble refusal, the luster of which is undimmed by the flight of time. Parents frequently name their daughters Esther. I wonder why they never use that noble name, Vashti. One of the things that would bless our country today would be a new kind of women's, or young women's, organization. We might call it, "The Order of Vashti," the order of those women who to the pagan practices and degrading customs of the present day have the courage to say no.

THE NO OF CHRIST

This is the no that brought man redemption and salvation. There were three memorable occasions when Christ uttered it. The first was when the Devil tempted Him in the wilderness and thrice sought to turn Him aside from the great work of redemption. To each proposal Christ answered with a mighty no. If He had failed there, He could never have been our Redeemer. John Milton, with appropriateness, brings "Paradise Regained" to a close, not with the crucifixion or the Resurrection, but with the Temptation.

The second time Jesus uttered that mighty no was when Satan came to Him in the Garden of Gethsemane and again sought to turn him back from the Cross. Again Christ answered no. "Nevertheless, not my will but Thine be done." And when the angels heard that no in Heaven, they came rushing down to crown Him and salute Him. So the evangelists tell us that "there appeared a great angel from Heaven, strengthening Him."

The third and last time Christ uttered that mighty no was on the Cross when the mob which stood about and the two thieves who hung at his side—both of them at first—mocked Him and taunted Him, and said, "If thou be the Christ, the Son of God, come down from the Cross! Save Thyself and us!" All Heaven and hell waited with breathless suspense to hear what Christ would answer. That answer was no. "It is finished." When Christ uttered that no, Satan was conquered and Heaven was opened for the sinner.

Christ told us that the great business of His followers is to say no. Deny thyself, take up thy cross, and say no to the temptations of self, of others, of the world. Are you just a drifter? Are you a weak yes man? The cure for that is to say no. Say yes to Christ, and then you will have the power to say no to the world. "Thou shalt say no!"

5

THE MEANEST WORD

A mean thing is that which is injurious to another person, and where the injury is wrought without any hurt or harm, or chance of it, to the person who inflicts the injury. Therefore, the meanest thing is both cowardly and cruel. In this sense, then, what is the meanest word?

What is the meanest word because it is the most cowardly word? What is the meanest word because it is the cruelest word? What is the word that is conceived in malignity and born in hatred? What is the word that many use lightly and carelessly, and yet thereby ally themselves with the cruel and cowardly man? What is the word that has destroyed friendships, disrupted churches, devastated homes, engendered war and strife, saddened and clouded the lives of men and women? What is the word that the Devil first used in the Garden of Eden when he spoke against God, and which he has employed ever since? What is the word that has broken more hearts than any other? What is the word that has the lowest and softest sound and accent, and yet the loudest and noisiest echo? That word is *whisperer*. "A whisperer separateth chief friends"—Proverbs 16:28.

The whisperer speaks all languages, wears all kinds of clothing, is a citizen of all countries, belongs to all political parties, moves in all circles, and is a member of all churches. Here again, as in the case of the other words, to prove our point that the whisperer is the meanest word we shall fall back on that wonderful book, the Bible, and see what evil the whisperer has done to man.

The world started on the wrong track, through the whispered innuendo of the Devil, who, Christ said, "was a liar and the father of lies from the beginning." The devil sowed the seeds of doubt and disobedience in the mind of the woman, first of all, by misrepresenting God, although he did it in the form of a question. "Yea, hath God said, ye shall not eat of every tree of the Garden?" That was not so. There was only one tree, the Tree of the Knowledge of Good and Evil, of which they were not permitted to eat. That earliest form of slander, misrepresentation, and exaggeration, is one that is still very common. The whole plan of Satan at the beginning was to misrepresent God as a despot and tyrant, whose decree was against the good of the man and the woman. Thousands have suffered from a like whisper of misrepresentation which caricatures the person who is slandered and creates a false impression as to his personality.

Nehemiah, the heroic builder of the wars at Jerusalem, was a victim of the whisperer. Indeed, that has often been the lot of the greatest men. He who gets his head above the crowd of mediocrity will be the target of abuse. He who climbs the highest mountain peaks in human achievement must look down on the scorn and hate of the men below.

On this historic occasion, when Nehemiah and his associates were rebuilding the walls of Jerusalem, he encountered malignant opposition from the chieftains of the tribes living in the vicinity of Jerusalem. The leaders among these were Sanballat, the Horonite; and Tobiah, the Ammonite; and Gashmu, the Arabian. They tried in every way to prevent the building of the walls. Their first weapon was ridicule. They told Nehemiah that his wall was a joke, that if even a fox went up on the wall he would break it down. Then they tried the threat of an armed attack, but Nehemiah armed all the workmen with a sword so that he who worked with a trowel had a sword girded to his thigh. Then they made a futile attempt to trap Nehemiah into a supposedly friendly conference where they could assassinate him.

As a last resort they tried to frighten him from his task by slander. They came to him with an open unsealed letter, the inference being that everyone was aware of its contents. In the letter was this statement: "It is reported among the heathen, and Gashmu saith it, that thou and the Jews think to rebel, for which cause thou buildest the wall that thou mayest be their king according to these words." This was a most serious charge, and a dangerous rumor to be afloat. But Nehemiah, instead of being frightened by the report and the whispered slander, denied it and denounced it to these crafty heathen and asked God for strength to complete his task. "So we built the wall."

Sanballat and Tobiah and Ezra and Zechariah, and Nehemiah himself, save for his inspiring memory, are dead and gone long ago. But this fellow, Gashmu, strangely enough, the author of "They say," is still alive. You will find him in ancient Jerusalem and in modern New York and Pittsburgh. He belongs to all races and nations and speaks all languages. He has many aliases, among which are the following: "They tell me," "Have you heard it?" "Do you think it could be true?" "Don't tell anyone else, but—" "This is off the record, but—" Yet Gashmu is always hard to locate. His name never appears in the telephone book or the city directory, and if you search for him at his last reported address it will be found that he has always moved somewhere else. Gashmu, therefore, is the sign and symbol of the talebearer, the defamer, the detractor, the slanderer, the whisperer.

Another notorious whisperer of the Old Testament was Doeg, the Edomite. In the Old Testament gallery you cannot find a more sinister countenance than that of Doeg.

David had fled from the court of Saul to Nob, where the tabernacle and the priests were. Disturbed at David's appearance, the priest Ahimelech asked David how it was that he had come alone. David told him a plausible untruth that he had come on business for the king, business so secret that none but himself and Saul might know it. The old priest was easily satisfied with this explanation and permitted David to eat of the shewbread. He also armed him with the mighty sword of Goliath, the very sword with which David had cut off the head of that giant in the vale of Elah. As David grasped the hilt with his two hands, and looked upon the shining blade, revived by the memory of his great feat, he exclaimed, "Give it to me; there is none like that!"

Thus armed and refreshed, David hastened to leave the house of the priest. But as he was going out he saw Doeg, the chief herdsman of Saul, leaning against a pillar, and the moment he saw him he knew that Doeg purposed evil in his heart. From Nob David fled to the court of Achish, the king of Gath, where he escaped detection and arrest by feigning madness and scrabbling on the doors of the gate.

After a futile pursuit of David, Saul in a rage summoned his advisers and courtiers and said to them, "Have all of you con- spired against me that none discloseth to me when my son maketh a league with the son of Jesse? And there is none of you that is sorry for me, nor discloseth unto me that my son has stirred up my servant against me to lie in wait as at this day." None of his court answered him, perhaps because David was a general favorite and they hoped he would escape the mad rage of Saul, perhaps because they feared further to anger Saul. But Doeg was present. He broke the silence by saying this, "I saw the son of Jesse come to Nob to Ahimelech, and he inquired of Jehovah for him and gave him victuals and armed him with the sword of Goliath the Philistine." In a transport of fury, and certain now that Ahimelech was a traitor, Saul ordered the aged priest brought before him, and thus accused him, "Why hast thou conspired against me, thou and the son of Jesse, in that thou hast given him bread and a sword, and hast inquired of God for him that he should rise up against me, to lie in wait, as at this day?"

Astounded and hurt at the charge of disloyalty, the old priest protested his innocence and said he had supposed that Saul would have been pleased that he had assisted the king's son-in- law in time of need. His words, no doubt, impressed all who heard him with their truthfulness. But Saul was in one of those moods when a man neither wants to hear nor will hear the truth. When none of his guards would lift their swords to strike down Ahimelech, Saul called upon Doeg to perform the cruel and sacrilegious act, and Doeg, nothing loath, out with his sword and slew Ahimelech and eighty-five of the priests that day.

Ahimelech fell a victim to the sword of slander. There thou liest, Ahimelech, thou priest of God, weltering in thy blood, and all thy house with thee, slain by the sword of slander, thou and many another since. Never more wilt thou inquire of God in man's behalf. Never more wilt thou offer the atoning sacrifice. Never more wilt thou put on the ephod and the breastplate and read the will of God and the destiny of man in the scintillation of the mystic jewels. Thy priestly race is run; thy holy invocations are ended. Not for crimes or sins of thine own didst thou perish, but for a fault laid upon thee by a lying tongue. Thy long years of unfaltering loyalty availed thee nothing, nothing thy guileless tongue and thy holy life. Slander named thee for her victim. Hadst thou been as chaste as ice, as pure as snow, yet hadst thou not escaped the whisperings of the slanderer. Thy starlike loyalty, thy zeal for God's holy house and for his king anointed but served to make thee a shining mark at which the wicked shot his arrows.

In a double sense Doeg was the assassin and murderer of the priest Ahimelech. He was a past master in the art of defamation of character. It was not what he said about Ahimelech that ruined the priest in Saul's regard, but what he insinuated. So far as what he said was concerned, everything was true. Abimelech had given David the shewbread to eat, and he had armed him with the great sword of Goliath. But Doeg did not tell Saul that the priest thought that David had come on an errand for the king. Doeg told Saul the truth, but not the whole truth, and the result was a slaughtered high priest and eighty-five others of the priesthood.

Doeg's slander was born of pure depravity and malignity. We shrink from accepting such a fact about the human heart, but it is sadly true. In the Letter to the Romans where he wishes to describe and illustrate and prove the depravity of the human heart, St. Paul speaks of men as backbiters, haters of God, and whisperers. David himself, who afterwards suffered so much at the hand of the whisperer and the slanderer, said of them, "They bend their bow in darkness, and under their tongue is the poison of asps." Just as the ichneumon destroys the crocodile's eggs, not because he wants to eat them, but out of a pure passion for destruction, so there are whisperers who injure and cloud the lives of men out of a pure desire for inflicting suffering and doing evil.

But the original whisperer and slanderer could make little headway or do little injury were he not able to enlist the assistance and service of many who repeat his whisper. This is possible only because of that sad trait in human nature which delights in hearing evil of others. There are, alas, many who rejoice in iniquity. So the wicked whisper is repeated, sometimes with an injunction that it is to go no further, and sometimes with an expression of mock sorrow or concern. This sorrow and concern is hypocritical, because if there were such genuine sorrow and concern it would prove itself by a refusal to repeat the whisper. There are not many men like Henry M. Stanley, who said he did not belong to that vile herd who always say, "Where there is so much smoke there must be a fire," and that he always reminded those who came to him with some evil tale against another man, that they knew less about the case than they had supposed.

Whoever listens with interest and delight to a slanderous tale is almost as guilty as the man who whispers the tale, and an old writer has said that both ought to be hanged, the whisperer by the tongue and the other by the ear.

It is difficult to overtake a whisper which quickly swells to a loud and raucous shout. Some years ago, when the character of a prominent man was being assailed, a number of men formed what they called the "Trace It Down Club." Their search showed that the evil report was pure calumny. In a multitude of cases this is so. But slander has a swift foot, and once started, it is almost impossible to overtake her. In her story of Amos Barton in "Scenes of Clerical Life," when evil surmises were made as to an innocent friendship, George Eliot thus describes the spread and the growth of the slander: "I can only ask my reader, Did you ever upset your ink bottle and watch in helpless agony the rapid spread of Stygian blackness over your fair manuscript or fairer table cover? With a like inky swiftness did gossip now blacken the reputation of Amos Barton, causing the unfriendly to scorn, and even the friendly to stand aloof at a time when difficulties of another kind were fast thickening around him."

The Old Testament description of the godly man still stands. "Who shall abide in thy tabernacle? Who shall dwell in thy holy hill? He that walketh uprightly and worketh righteousness and speaketh the truth in his heart, he that backbiteth not in his tongue, nor doeth evil against his neighbor, nor taketh up reproach against his neighbor." In the New Testament the beautiful sketch of the perfect Christian gentleman is found in the thirteenth chapter of 1 Corinthians, where he is described as the man who "thinketh no evil, and rejoiceth not in iniquity." The true Christian will always seek to feel another's woe and hide the fault he sees. In the Royal Gallery in London, there is a portrait of himself by Salvatora Rosa. In his right hand he holds a placard on which are written in Latin these words, "Either keep silence, or speak things better than silence."

> If you are tempted to reveal
> A tale someone to you has told
> About another, make it pass,
> Before you speak, three gates of gold—
> Three narrow gates: first, 'Is it true?'
> Then 'Is it needful?' In your mind
> Give truthful answer. And the next
> Is last and narrowest: 'Is it kind?'
> And if, to reach your lips at last,
> It passes through these gateways three,
> Then you may tell the tale, nor fear
> What the result of speech may be.
>
> —Author Unknown

There is a kind of gossip that is good and profitable. One of the turning points in the early life of John Bunyan was when he chanced to hear three or four poor women sitting at a door in the sun, talking about the things of God. If they had been talking about their neighbors or rolling some morsel of scandal under their tongues, who knows that it might not have been altogether different in the future with John Bunyan. But what he heard them talking about was the New Birth, the work of God in their hearts, and how they were comforted and refreshed by the love of Christ. As he went about his work as a tinker, mending the pots and pans of the neighborhood, "their talk and discourse went with him."

That is the right kind of gossip. Let us whisper and speak the great things that God hath done for us in Christ. Will your intimate and friendly talk be such as will encourage and help others and guide them into the way of peace?

6

GOD'S FAVORITE WORD

What is God's favorite word? What is the word that echoes with sweet music in every part of the Bible? What was the word that God spake to man before He destroyed the earth with a flood? What is the word that prophets and apostles like to pronounce? What is the word that brought Peter to Jesus? What is the word that was so often upon the lips of Christ? What is the word that He spoke to little children, and to the weary and the heavy laden? What is the word which, obeyed, awakens joy among the angels in heaven? What is the word which, disobeyed, brings sorrow to the heart of Christ? What is the word that brings the Bible to a close and strikes its final chord of music? What is the word which is inscribed in letters of gold over the gates of heaven, those gates to which the guardian angels of the souls of men are ever pointing their pilgrim feet?

That word is *come*. One could delete from the Bible all other passages, and yet with those great passages which pronounce the word "come" there would be a full Gospel to preach. There are commandments and judgments and denunciations in the Bible, for God is a God of righteousness and truth, but sounding like a haunting refrain in and above and through all other voices is the voice of invitation, come. If you leave me just that one word come, just that one string in my lyre, still I can sing the whole story of redemption and vie with the angels themselves. Come is the great word of the Gospel. Go is the great word of the law. The law shows the gulf between God and the sinner. The Gospel bridges that gulf. The law drives; the Gospel leads. Christ ever goes before, as a Shepherd before His flock. Here again we can prove that come is God's favorite word by its use in the Bible.

NOAH AND THE FLOOD

Noah stands high in the list of the saviors of mankind. He comes upon the stage at a great crisis in the history of the race. The whole earth was corrupt before God. When we see what is going on in the world today we wonder how it could be much more corrupt than the world of our day. But we must remember that the wickedness and apostasy of our own generation, terrible though that is, is relieved by the godly living and the earnest prayer and pleading of those who are faithful to God. Everywhere over the earth today prayers of intercession and of repentance go up to heaven. Were it not for that, God might indeed destroy the earth with a flood. Not only were the actions of men corrupt, but the fountain of human action, thought, and imagination was defiled. "And God saw that the wickedness of man was great on the earth, and that every imagination of the thoughts of his heart was only evil continually." Because of this universal wickedness, God's fiat went forth for the destruction of the world. Noah was commanded to build an ark in order that he might save himself, and others who were willing to be saved, from the deluge which was to judge mankind. In the prompt obedience of Noah, and that in spite of scoffing and ridicule, we have one of the greatest examples of faith recorded in the Bible. Ages afterwards it was not forgotten, for the inspired writer who built with his pen the world's greatest hall of fame, the eleventh chapter of the Letter to the Hebrews, says of Noah: "By faith Noah, being warned of God of things not seen as yet, moved with fear, prepared an ark to the saving of his house, by the which he condemned the world and became heir of the righteousness which is by faith."

When the ark was finished, God said to Noah, "Come thou and all thy house into the ark." Then, when Noah and his family had taken refuge, "floods prevailed exceedingly over the earth, and all the high hills under the whole heaven were covered, and all flesh died that moved upon the earth; all in whose nostrils was the breath of life and every living substance was destroyed which was upon the face of the ground, both man and cattle and the creeping things and the fowl of the heaven. And Noah only remained alive and they that were with him in the ark." Death! Death! Universal death!

If you go into the Catacombs at Rome today, those narrow tunnels where the early Christians laid away their dead, one of the pictures that you will see most frequently, as a symbol of their Christian hope and faith, is that of the ark floating upon the face of the waters. The ark was the symbol of the Church. Still the Church floats upon the good of the world's judgment and the world's iniquity, and still the ambassador of God says to the sons of men, "Come into the ark, thou and thy house." We must have the highest views of the Church of Christ as God's plan. Make no apology for it, no defense of it, but say to a perishing world what God said in the beginning, "Come into the ark." When we invite men to come into the Church, remember this is not a man's word; it is not the minister's invitation, but God's. With that invitation, with that word, "Come," the history of redemption begins and closes. God said to Noah, when the flood destroyed the world, "Come into the ark," and in the Apocalypse, when the long battle with sin and darkness is over, John heard the voice of God saying, "Come; the Spirit and the Bride say, come."

CHRIST AND BARTIMAEUS

It was a bright spring morning at Jericho. Blind Bartimaeus finds a sunny spot against the wall and waits to see what the day will bring him. As he sits there he hears in the distance the hum of voices and the shuffling of feet. His trained ear lets him know that it was more than the usual street procession and traffic which was coming. When those who were in advance of the procession were hurrying by, Bartimaeus stretched out his hand and seizing one of them by his skirt said to him, "What is it all about? What is the stir? What is the excitement?" The man, freeing his garment and hurrying on, answered, "Jesus of Nazareth passeth by!" "Jesus of Nazareth!" thought the beggar to himself. I have heard of him before. Some say he is a good man; some say that he is an impostor and bad man. But I have heard that He is able to do great miracles, and that He has even opened the eyes of a blind man. If He was able to do that for another blind man, why not for me? With hope kindling in his heart, Bartimaeus sits silent until his practiced ear lets him know that the center of the procession is at hand. Then, lifting up his voice, he cries out, in a tone that is heard above the murmur and hubbub of the passing multitude, "Jesus of Nazareth, thou Son of David, have mercy on me!"

The cry was so loud and piercing that none in the vicinity could have failed to hear it. Other beggars or blind men sitting near Bartimaeus at the gate, perhaps frightened at his outcry, said to him, "Keep still, Bartimaeus! If you shout like that, the magistrates will have us all beaten and cast into prison." I suppose, too, that more important persons joined in the indignant chorus of rebuke. Probably the Pharisees and leaders of the people, whose official welcome had been rudely interrupted by the cry of Bartimaeus, gave orders to have him silenced. Peter, James, or John may have had something to say in addition. It's a bad thing not to come to Christ ourselves, but a worst thing to stand in the way of others. If you will not come yourself, be sure that you do not hinder others.

But the more the bystanders rebuked Bartimaeus, the louder rose his piercing cry, "Jesus of Nazareth, have mercy on me." Hearing the cry, Jesus stood still. Many other shouts and voices were going up, but that was the one Jesus heard. "And Jesus stood still." Omnipotence stops on its way to hear the cry of human sorrow and misery. Jesus of Nazareth is always passing by, and yet for some, too, He is always standing still.

The moment Jesus stopped, the chief men of the town began to make explanation and apology. "This is only one of our town beggars. We had given strict orders that all beggars be removed from the street, and we are sorry that—" But Jesus broke in on their apologies, by saying, "Call him; tell him to come to me." They looked in blank astonishment for a moment, and then seeing that He meant it, hurried towards the place where Bartimaeus was sitting. Now that Jesus had recognized him and called him, all those who had been angrily telling Bartimaeus to keep still now changed their tone. Now they are all showing courtesy and kindness. "Here," said one, "is your garment." And another, "Here is your staff." And another, "Give me your hand, and I'll help you to your feet." But refusing their assistance, Bartimaeus sprang to his feet, and casting his garment away from him lest it should impede him, he ran all by himself in the direction where Christ was. What a scene! Jesus, the Light of the world, standing still, and the blind beggar all atremble and all excited, standing before him!

Jesus knew what he wanted, and yet he said to him, "What wilt thou that I should do unto thee?" What was the wish and will of Bartimaeus? Did he say, "Lord, that thou shouldest take these rags from me and clothe me in a fine raiment"? Or, "Lord, that thou shouldest take me off the street and put me in a fine house"? Or, "Lord, that thou shouldest make me a ruler over the people"? No, that was not what the blind beggar asked. What he asked was this, "Lord, that I may receive my sight. I want to see. I want to see the sky that men tell me is so blue, and the hills of Moab beyond the Jordan and the Dead Sea, and the Temple of God in Jerusalem. Lord, restore unto me my sight! Open my eyes." Then Jesus said to him, "Go thy way, thy faith hath made thee whole."

The word come is not used here, except when it is said that the beggar came to Jesus. But that is what Jesus asked him to do. He called for him to come to him, and the beggar came. There are three things that the beggar did here: he called, he ran; he believed and saw. And there are three things that Jesus did here, and that He is still doing: He was passing by, He stood still, and He called for Bartimaeus to come to Him. Jesus of Nazareth passeth by! This was the last time that Jesus ever went through Jericho. If Bartimaeus had not called, if he had not come to Christ that morning, his eyes would never have been opened. Always for someone Jesus of Nazareth is passing by for the last time. For some tonight he is passing through Pittsburgh for the last time. He is passing through the

First Church on this Sunday night for the last time. Once again He stands still! More wonderful than when the sun stood still in heaven! And He sends this message, "Call him unto Me." Christ tells you to come.

THE LAST COME OF THE BIBLE

We have not time for some of those other beautiful comes of Christ and the Bible: His beautiful word to little children, "Suffer the little children to come unto me and forbid them not, for of such is the Kingdom of Heaven"; His earnest, tender, come, to the rich young ruler, who asked him the way of Eternal Life and to whom He said, "One thing thou lackest, go, sell whatsoever thou hast, and give to the poor and thou shalt have treasure in heaven, and come, follow me," or His tender and beautiful word to all those who labor and are heavy laden, "Come unto me, and I will give you rest." But all those great comes, and all the music of come as it echoes and re-echoes in the Bible, are summed up in that final invitation, the invitation that brings to a close all the words and all the invitations of the Bible—"The Spirit and the Bride say, come, and let him that heareth say, come, and let him that is athirst come, and whosoever will, let him take of the water of life freely."

Water is man's great necessity. Without it no child can thrive, no nation can exist. What is the word that you hear from the lips of the traveler lost on the face of the scorched desert? Water. What is the word that you hear on the lips of the sick and feverish man as he tosses on his bed? Water. What is the piteous appeal and murmur that you hear on the lips of the wounded in battle as they lie on the field of carnage? Water. How beautiful, then, is this metaphor, the Water of Life! As the body must have water, so the soul must have the Water of Life. The Bible closes with an invitation to drink of that water. The invitation takes in everyone. Whosoever will, let him take of the Water of Life.

> None are excluded hence,
> But those who do themselves exclude.
>
> —Author Unknown

There is only one condition, and that is that you take it freely. It is the most valuable thing in the universe, but there is no price that you can offer for it. You have no money with which you can buy it. "Come ye to the waters, yea, come, buy wine and milk without money and without price."

Come, then, is God's favorite word to man. It was spoken first to man when he, at the flood, said to Noah, "Come into the ark." And when for the salvation and redemption of mankind God has sent prophets and apostles, has worked great miracles, given the law and the Gospel, sent Christ, the express image of His person, to speak to men, to die for them on the Cross, to rise again from the dead and ascend into heaven, there to make intercession for man; after all the providences and all the judgments, and all the revelations of all the ages, God sums it all up in this one word, so beautiful, so full of tenderness and love and compassion, come. "The Spirit and the Bride say, come; and let him that heareth say come, and let him that is athirst come; and whosoever will let him come and take of the Water of Life freely." May God's great and beautiful come be answered tonight by some penitent and returning soul.

> Just as I am, without one plea,
> But that Thy blood was shed for me,
> And that Thou bidd'st me come to Thee,
> O Lamb of God, I come!
>
> —Charlotte Elliott

7

THE MOST DANGEROUS WORD

Some thought it was hate; others hell; and others fear, rumor, revenge, or Death. But it is a less dangerous looking and a less dangerous sounding word than any of these. Indeed, that is the dangerous thing about this word: it hides and disguises the threat and menace that are in it. What is the most dangerous word? What is the word that has closed the door of success to many a dreamer and condemned him who pronounces it to failure, penury, and woe? What is the word that paralyzes action and leaves duty undone? What is the word that is one of the easiest to speak, and at the same time one of the most fatal in its effect? What is the word that shines like a mirage on the desert's face and deceives the pilgrim with its false promise? What is the word that burns and shines like an *ignis fatuus* before the deluded eyes of man? What is the word that has lighted fools the way to dusty death? What is the word above all others that Satan likes to persuade men to use, and therefore is Satan's favorite word? What is the word that has shut the gate of the Kingdom of Heaven and condemned souls to outer darkness? What is the word that more than any other keeps men from coming to Christ? That word is *tomorrow*. "Boast not thyself of tomorrow"— Proverbs 27:1.

> Tomorrow, and tomorrow, and tomorrow,
> Creeps in this petty pace from day to day,
> To the last syllable of recorded time;

And all our yesterdays have lighted fools
The way to dusty death.

—Shakespeare, *Macbeth*

"Go to, ye that say tomorrow, for ye know not what shall be on the morrow" (James 4:13, 14). As one takes a pleasing opiate and sinks into slumber, so tomorrow casts its spell over the energies of man. That tomorrow is the most dangerous of all words, is a self-evident truth. Yet, as in the case of the other words, we prove our point again by illustration from the lives of men in the Bible. The great word of the Bible is always today. "Boast not thyself of tomorrow," and again, "The Holy Ghost saith, today." The Bible and the Holy Spirit never say sometimes, but always now; never tomorrow, but always today.

ABSALOM'S TOMORROW

Here we have an instance of how the policy of tomorrow proved dangerous and fatal to Absalom. Absalom had rebelled against his father David and driven him out of Jerusalem. As David fled with his followers towards the country beyond the Jordan, it was told him that Ahithophel was one of the co-conspirators and was a counselor to Absalom. David knew Ahithophel for a wise and crafty man, and the moment he heard that he was in the camp of Absalom, David uttered the prayer, "O Lord, I pray Thee, turn the counsel of Ahithophel into foolishness."

The answer to David's prayer came in the person of another counselor and friend, Hushai, the Archite, who joined David and his party in their flight from Jerusalem. Instead of taking Hushai with him, David told him to return to Jerusalem, attach himself to Absalom, and, if possible, defeat the counsel of Ahithophel. When Hushai appeared at the court of Absalom and cried, "God save the King," Absalom, knowing his former friendship for David, was somewhat suspicious, and said to Hushai, "Is this thy kindness to thy friend? Why wentest thou not with thy friend?" To this Hushai answered that he was now the friend and counselor of Absalom, and that he would serve him as faithfully as he had served David. Thus deceived and taken in, Absalom attached Hushai to his staff.

In the meantime, Absalom had sought the counsel of Ahithophel, who had the real interests of Absalom at heart. Ahithophel counseled him, first, to commit a deed of turpitude and shame in connection with David's household and wives which would make Absalom and all his followers abhorred of David, and render impossible a reconciliation. Then he advised Absalom to let him take 12,000 veteran troops, and with these men he would pursue and overtake David that very night. "And I will come upon him when he is weary and weak-handed, and will make him afraid. And all the people that are with him shall flee, and I will smite the king only, and I will bring back all the people to thee." This wise counsel, wise so far as the interests of Absalom were concerned, pleased that handsome rebel and blackguard and all the elders of Israel who were with him. Had Ahithophel's counsel been followed, there is no doubt that David and his army would have been destroyed.

But before following the counsel of Ahithophel, Absalom summoned Hushai and asked him what he had to advise. The crafty Hushai reminded Absalom that David and his followers were mighty men of war, and that David now would be like a bear robbed of her whelps in the field. It would be rash and foolish to attack him until they knew his exact position and the strength of the army that was with him, for, said Hushai, if Absalom's pursuing army met with a temporary reverse, and the rumor went abroad that there had been a slaughter among the people that followed Absalom, it might have a disastrous effect upon Absalom's cause. Therefore, Hushai counseled Absalom not to pursue David at once, but first of all, to recruit a great army out of all Israel from Dan to Beersheba, and when the army had been assembled, to lead them out himself to battle against David. "So shall we come upon him in some place where he shall be found, and we will light upon him as the dew shall fall upon the ground, and of him and of all the men that are with him there shall not be left as much as one."

Deceived by the eloquent plausibility of Hushai, Absalom decided to follow this foolish counsel, instead of at once attacking David, as Ahithophel had advised. When Ahithophel saw what the decision was, knowing that it would be fatal, both to the cause of Absalom and to his own safety, he hurried to his home and hanged himself in chagrin and despair.

The foolish counsel of Hushai, which Absalom, thinking it was sincere, had adopted, with its delay of several days, gave David and his captains full time to organize his army, and when Absalom and his host came marching against David in the Wood of Ephraim they were easily and quickly overthrown by David's veterans. Absalom in retreat from the battle was caught in the branches of an oak by his luxurious hair and slain by the hand of Joab, David's captain of the host. His body was cast into a pit, and when the battle was over, the soldiers of David's army threw stones into the pit as they marched past it, and with each stone a curse, until a great pile of stones had been raised over the spot where Absalom's once beautiful body lay.

We are all glad that it was Absalom who was over-thrown and defeated and not David. But the point we make is that by the fatal counsel of tomorrow, Absalom and his army were destroyed. In the king's dale Absalom had reared for himself a costly pillar or mausoleum. There he expected to be laid away in his royal robes. But this beautiful tomb was a tomb without a tenant, a pillar without a prince, a monument without a man. Instead of resting in that marble mausoleum, the gashed and mutilated body of Absalom lay at the bottom of a pit in the forest, covered with stones and curses, and with none save his broken-hearted father to mourn over him. Thus, tomorrow, with its crafty deception, frustrates hope and destroys ambition. Coming out of the Wood of Ephraim, I paused by the pile of stones that mark the grave of Absalom, and on one of those stones I read Absalom's epitaph. It was this: "Tomorrow." If you have anything good or worthy that you would like to do, any tender work that ought to be done, now is the time to do it. Boast not thyself of tomorrow, for tomorrow may never come.

FELIX AND HIS TOMORROW

Paul had preached a great sermon that day to Felix, the governor of Judaea. With Felix was the lovely Jewess, Drusilla, a daughter of Herod Agrippa. She had first married a Gentile, who, to please her, had become a Jew. Then Felix, with the aid of a sorcerer's incantations, had won her from her husband and was living with her in sin and shame. All that was dishonorable in mankind and in human nature was represented by that combination of Felix and Drusilla as they sat together on the throne while Paul preached to them. Felix was waiting for more information about this prisoner, Paul, and to while away the time he had invited Paul to preach a sermon to him and to his consort Drusilla.

It was a memorable sermon that Paul preached. He preached as all ministers ought to preach—

> As never sure to preach again,
> And as a dying man to dying men.

The sermon had three heads. Paul reasoned with Felix of righteousness, temperance, and judgment to come. As Paul reasoned of righteousness, Felix and Drusilla, no doubt, looked at one another in surprise. Instead of a half hour's entertainment, or the relationship of Christianity to Judaism, or some mysterious and recondite subject, Paul talked to Felix and his wife about righteousness, and as he did so their wicked past rose before them to condemn them. Then he preached and reasoned on temperance, or self control. Drusilla must have been very uncomfortable as she recalled her shameful escapades and her adulterous union with Felix. Then came the thrilling climax to the sermon, judgment to come. Paul did not leave that out the way so many preachers do today. He preached not only to the times, but to the eternities, and made it clear to Felix and Drusilla that although now they sat on the throne and judged and examined others, the day was coming when they must appear before the judgment seat of Christ.

This powerful sermon had a great effect on Felix. Indeed, what happened was one of the greatest triumphs ever achieved by a preacher. This sated sensualist and cruel pagan had his conscience stirred. "Felix trembled." He had a vision of the judgment, a vision of God. He was in a mood when he might have repented and turned back to God and to a righteous way of life. But, instead of acting upon his conviction and his emotion, Felix told Paul that at a more convenient season he would hear from him again. "Go thy way for this time. When I have a convenient season I will call for thee." And Felix did call for Paul, and heard him preach frequently, but never again did Paul's preaching produce the same effect in the heart of Felix. Never again did Felix tremble. The tragedy of it was that in the end Felix tried to make use of Paul, who once had roused his conscience, as a man from whom he might get something in the way of a bribe. Thus Felix's last state was worse than his first. On his tomb is the epitaph, tomorrow.

It is never safe to say tomorrow when God says today. Tomorrow may mean Goodbye to God. The reasons for this are twofold: First, the uncertainty of life. How powerfully that is put by St. James, where he says, "Go to now, ye that say today or tomorrow will we go into such a city and continue there a year and buy and sell and get gain; whereas ye know not what shall be on the morrow. For what is your life? It is even a vapor that appeareth for a little time and then vanisheth away." Who can count on tomorrow? In the Bible there are eighteen or more metaphors which express the brevity, the transitoriness, and the uncertainty of life. Among these are, "The shadow that declineth," "Water spilt on the ground," "The weaver's shuttle," "The swift ship," seen now, then lost on the horizon, the vapor or the mist of the morning which disappears before the sun. How true that is! Therefore, say not, tomorrow.

The other reason why it is never safe to say tomorrow is that the soul has its favorable moments, and God has His acceptable time. The man who is stirred and moved tonight may hear without interest and without emotion the same truth next Sunday night. Felix said he would hear Paul at a more convenient season, and frequently, when he thought that convenient season had come, he called for Paul to preach to him. But now the preaching that once made Felix tremble no longer stirs him. His hour had passed. To how many of life's most precious opportunities, and to the greatest opportunity of all, the opportunity to repent and to believe on Christ men say, "Tomorrow." "Go thy way. When I have a more convenient season, I will call for thee." And then tomorrow comes, but, alas, it is always yesterday.

THE RICH FOOL'S TOMORROW

Here is a man, just like the one described by St. James, who announced what he was going to do tomorrow. Indeed, he counted on a great many tomorrows, for when he planned to pull down his barns and build greater and bestow all his fruits and his goods, he thus soliloquized with his soul: "Soul, thou hast much goods laid up for many years. Take thine ease, eat, drink, and be merry." But when he had finished this speech, with its boastful anticipation of many selfish and sinful tomorrows, then God began to speak. "Thou fool! This night thy soul shall be required of thee. Then whose shall those things be which thou hast provided?"

The night passed, the day dawned, tomorrow came. It was one of those tomorrows on which the rich fool had counted so much. But now all that tomorrow meant to him was death, for on the morrow they wrapped him in a shroud and laid him in his grave. Those fields, his barns bursting with plenty, and all his possessions, all that he had to leave behind him. On his grave, too, is that epitaph, tomorrow.

When we say, "Boast not thyself of tomorrow," we do not mean that a man is not to take wise forethought for tomorrow. Any worthy life must plan nobly for tomorrow. Most of the blessings of civilization and liberty which we enjoy are fruit sown by men who thought about tomorrow. We should all plan for greater things, statelier mansions, a nobler life, tomorrow, and a life tomorrow that is better than today's. But no one can boast of tomorrow. No one can count on tomorrow. How many good things were going to be done tomorrow, but were never done, for tomorrow was always one day ahead, or always one day behind—yesterday.

He was going to be all that a mortal should be
    Tomorrow
No one would be better than he
    Tomorrow

Each morning he stacked up the letters he'd write
    Tomorrow
It was too bad indeed he was too busy to see Bill, but he promised to do it
    Tomorrow
The greatest of workers this man would have been
    Tomorrow
The world would have known him had be ever seen
    Tomorrow
But the fact is he died and faded from view, and all that was left
when living was through
Was a mountain of things he intended to do
    Tomorrow

—Author Unknown

No one should omit to do a kindness today on the theory that he will do it tomorrow. No one should leave until tomorrow the breaking of a chain of some evil habit, and most of all, no one should leave until tomorrow repentance and faith in Christ. Say tomorrow to any one, to any invitation, but not to Christ, and not to Eternal Life.

In the mountains of West Virginia at one of the county seats there is the equestrian statue of a well-known Christian statesman. On it are these words: "He worked as if he would live forever; he lived as if he would die tomorrow."

8

THE MOST MYSTERIOUS WORD

What is the most mysterious word? Some thought it was death, and others eternity. But it is a word nearer to us than death or eternity. What is the most mysterious word? What is the word, that if we knew its answer, we would know as much as God? What is the word that righteous souls who believe in God and in God's government of the world have spoken as they looked out over the world and saw the reign of injustice and wickedness? What is the word that believing and afflicted souls have pronounced when God's hand lay heavy upon them? What is the word that mothers have spoken as they stood by the lifeless form of their children? What is the word that Gideon spoke when he saw Israel devastated by the Midianites? What is the word that Job uttered when the Lord stripped him of his possessions, took his sons and daughters away in death, and left him naked and desolate on an ash heap? What is the word that the Psalmist spoke when he thought that God had forgotten him? What is the word for the answer to which we shall have to wait till the gates of heaven are opened? What is the word that sums up the inscrutable mystery of human life? What is the word that fell from the lips of Christ when there was thick darkness over the face of the earth and He hung dying upon the Cross?

That word is *why*. "Why, then, has all this befallen us?"—Judges 6:13. Why is one of the first words that our infant lips pronounce, one of the last words that we speak after life's experience is over. Why is the word of a little child, and also the word of the tottering octogenarian. That why is the most mysterious word in the Bible and in human speech, and that it is a symbol of the unknown and the unknowable in human life and experience, we can demonstrate by illustration from the lives of those men in the Bible upon whose lips we hear this word of mystery.

GIDEON'S WHY

The land of Israel lay under the iron heel of the Midianites. Every summer they came raiding in from the country beyond the Jordan to devour the harvest which the Israelites had gathered. None dared to thresh his grain openly, for that would have invited the hand of the spoiler. In a hidden glen under the oak at Ophrah, a young man, Gideon, was secretly threshing out the grain of his father's farm. He was not threshing with oxen, as you can still see them doing in Palestine, for the lowing of the animals would have revealed the hidden threshing floor to the Midianites, but was beating out the grain by hand with a flail, and as he beat the grain his heart was hot and heavy over the plight of his country.

As Gideon was thus occupied, a stranger suddenly accosted him, standing by the oak under the shade of which he was beating out the grain. The stranger said to him, "The Lord is with thee, thou mighty man of valor." At this Gideon looked up with incredulity and astonishment upon his face and replied, "O my Lord, if the Lord be with us, why then has all this befallen us? And where be all His miracles which our fathers told us of, saying, 'Did not the Lord bring us up from Egypt?' But now the Lord hath forsaken us and delivered us into the hand of the Midianites."

It was as if Gideon had answered, "The Lord is with me! It certainly looks like it, doesn't it! Here I am, compelled to beat out a pitiful harvest on this secret threshing floor. The same is true all over our country. Look you! From the opening of this glen you can see a vast stretch of the plain of Esdraelon. Once from a thousand threshing floors you could see the yellow dust going up like smoke to heaven. But now you cannot see a single threshing floor. The Midianites have swept it clean. And worse than that, the false worship of the conquerors has invaded the land. There is a grove of Baal and an altar of Baal even in front of my father's house. God with me, indeed! If God is with us and with our country, then why has all this happened to us? Why does God let the Midianites invade our land and devour its substance? I have heard my father and my grandfather tell of the mighty miracles which God wrought in the past, how He delivered our people with a mighty hand out of the land of Egypt, smiting the firstborn of Egypt, cleaving a way for Israel through the Red Sea, leading them by a pillar of cloud by day and a pillar of fire by night. But now it looks as if either God did not care for His people, or, if He does care, that He is not able to do for them what He did in the past."

Why hath all this befallen us? This question asked by Gideon of the angel of the Lord at his secret threshing floor is one which has never ceased to echo through the world. We hear the echo of it as men look out today upon the state of the country, of the world, and of the church of Christ. "If God is with us, why hath all this befallen us?"

It is not many years ago that we were hoping that after the devastation and ruin of the World War that the nations would learn the more excellent way of peace, and would come to deal with one another on the principles of justice and brotherly good will. But now what do we see in the world? We see the nations armed as never before and the heavens illuminated with the sparks that fly from the grindstone of Mars. The nations hold their breath, dreading, and yet expecting, another inundation of violence and blood. Instead of being discredited and cast aside, the rule of dominion by force seems to be stronger than ever, and in Europe and on the continent of Asia we contemplate the cruel tragedies of violence and brute force. What wonder, then, that some should ask, if God's Holy Spirit is in the world, and if God presides over the destinies of men and nations, why hath all this befallen the world?

The same question is on our lips when we look at the church of Christ upon the earth. It is still rent by schisms and still distressed by heresies. At the very time when there was greater need than ever before for faith in the Bible as the oracle of God, we find everywhere questioning as to the truth and authority of the Scriptures. At the very time when Christians by their lives should show the aloofness and unworldliness of the Kingdom of God, there is an increasing lowering of the standards of Christian conduct and a closer and closer conformity to the world. At the very time when of all times in the history of the Church her members should witness to the world by showing their loyalty to the Church and to its services, we behold increasing disloyalty and indifference. The earnest Christian will say within his soul, "Why, O God, hath all this befallen Thy Church? How long, O Lord, how long?"

The remarkable thing in the history of Gideon is that when he asked this question of the angel, "Why hath all this befallen us," the angel did not answer him, or rather, his only answer was this: "The Lord looked upon him and said, Go in this thy might, and thou shalt save Israel from the hand of the Midianites. Have not I sent thee?" Gideon had been looking at the state of his father's house, at the state of his native land, swarming with the hordes of the Midianites. But now the Lord looked upon Gideon, and Gideon looked upon the Lord. Courage came to nerve his aim, and ere long the blare of three hundred trumpets, the crash of three hundred pitchers, and the flash of three hundred lights proclaimed the overthrow of Midian and the deliverance of the people of Israel.

In other words, God's answer to Gideon's why, to his troubled question about the state of his country and the state of religion, was a command to action. That is God's answer to you and me when we ask the question of Gideon. Our part is to take our place in the ranks of those who stand for the truth and who fight for God. Nothing is gained by sitting down and asking why things are thus.

> Stand up, stand up for Jesus,
> Each soldier to his post,
> Close up the broken column,
> And shout through all the host,
> Make good the loss so heavy
> In those that still remain,

And prove to all around you
That death itself is gain.

—Rev. George Duffield

JOB'S WHY

Job is the eternal symbol of the mystery of human life and the providence of God. "There was a man in the land of Uz whose name was Job and the man was perfect and upright and one that feared God and eschewed evil, and there were born unto him seven sons and three daughters. His substance also was seven thousand sheep and three thousand camels and five hundred yoke of oxen and five hundred she asses and a very great household, so that this man was the greatest of all the men of the east."

There you have Job—upright, renowned, blessed with sons and daughters and prosperous, the greatest man in the east. This is the man who is to be put to the severest trial. There came a day when the sons of God came to present themselves before the Lord, and Satan came also among them. And the Lord said unto Satan, "Whence comest thou?" Satan answered, "From going to and fro in the earth, from walking up and down in it." And the Lord said unto Satan, "Hast thou considered my servant Job, that there is none like him in the earth, a perfect and an upright man, one that feareth God and escheweth evil." To this Satan said with a sneer, "Doth Job fear God for naught?" The world is always ready to impute ulterior motives to any profession of faith and piety. So Satan mocked at the piety of Job. He said to the Lord, "Hast thou not made an hedge about him and about all his house, and all that he hath on every side? You have protected him from the storms and adversities of life. But now put forth thine hand and touch all that he hath, and he will curse thee to thy face."

God answered the blasphemous challenge of Satan by giving him permission, for even Satan in his work is under the authority of God, to test the righteousness of Job. Satan had Job in his power and had permission to take from him all his possessions, but he was not to touch Job himself.

Now swift calamities fall one after the other upon the

possessions and household of Job. First came a messenger to Job telling him that the Sabeans had driven off his thousand oxen and his five hundred asses and had slain the servants with the sword. The first messenger had hardly finished his melancholy tale when another arrived to tell Job that fire had fallen from heaven and burned up all his sheep and the shepherds attending them. The second messenger had hardly finished his tale when a third came and said that the Chaldeans had driven off Job's three thousand camels and slain their drivers with the swords. This third messenger had hardly finished his tale of woe when a fourth came with the sad tidings that a whirlwind had struck the house of Job's eldest son, where all his sons and daughters and their families were making merry, and all of them had perished in the collapse of the house.

Yesterday Job was the greatest and richest man of all the east. Today he is a pauper. Yesterday, he had seven sons and three daughters; now he has none to carry his name down to posterity. In a single day all his possessions, his prosperity, his family, had been swept away. When Job heard the dismal tidings, he arose and rent his mantle and shaved his head and fell down on the ground and worshipped, and said in those terms of resignation which smitten and stricken souls from age to age have used, "Naked came I out of my mother's womb, and naked shall I return thither. The Lord gave and the Lord has taken away. Blessed be the name of the Lord." Job had stood the first test of Satan successfully. "In all this Job sinned not, nor charged God foolishly."

But a second and more dangerous test was to follow. The sons of God again presented themselves in heaven, and Satan also was among them. When God asked Satan again about Job and said, "Still he holdeth fast his integrity, although thou movedest me against him to destroy him without cause," Satan answered with a sneer, "Skin for skin, yea," all that a man hath will he give for his life. But put forth thine hand now and touch his bone and his flesh and he will curse thee to thy face." In other words, Satan said that although Job had been able to retain his faith in God despite the loss of his property and his family, he would not do so if God smote him in his own body.

With God's permission to smite Job's body, but to spare his

life, Satan went forth from the presence of the Lord and smote Job with terrible boils from the sole of his foot to his crown. So terrible was his plight that even Job's wife, when she saw him sitting there on the ash pile scraping his diseased and filthy body with a potsherd, advised him to curse God and die. But again Job stood the test, and answered in words of magnificent resignation, "What? Shall we receive good at the hand of God and shall we not receive evil?"

But this does not mean that Job was not troubled in mind and distressed in soul. His three friends, Eliphas and Bildad and Zophar, came from afar to comfort him and mourn with him. With beautiful courtesy and understanding they sat seven days and seven nights in silence by his side when they saw that his grief was great. How great it was Job tells us. He opened his mouth and cursed the day that he was born. He did not curse the Lord, but he cursed the day that he was born and regretted that he had to face the battle and bear the burden of life. Then comes Job's great why: "Why died I not from the womb?" And thus he goes on, wondering why God gives life to man when life is capable of such pain of body and agony of soul. Why cannot men die when they long for death and dig for it more than hidden treasure? Why is light given to a man whose way is hidden?

Thus Job voiced the deepest sorrow and the sorest agony and the profoundest doubt of the life of man. That is the theme of this great drama of Job with its magnificent and sublime eloquence. All the deep why of mankind surges and echoes through the pages of this book, where the giant sufferer and the giant believer pours out his soul.

And what is the answer? There is no answer. Job's three friends, nor eloquent Elihu, nor Job himself could give the answer. And when God answered out of the whirlwind, He gave no answer to the deep, deep questions which Job in his agony had asked. Yet Job was not left desolate. God gave him faith, and after all, faith is the greatest answer. After his plaintive cry, and after his futile quest for the reason of things, Job comforts himself with this thought, "But He knoweth the way that I take, and when he hath tried me I shall come forth as gold." All that we can do is to put our trust in God and have faith that when he has tried us we shall come forth as gold.

> I know there are no errors
> In the great eternal plan,
> And all things work together
> For the final good of man.
> And I know when my soul speeds onward
> In its grand eternal quest,
> I shall say as I look back earthward,
> "Whatever is—is best.
>
> —Ella Wheeler Wilcox

OUR SAVIOR'S WHY

This is the most mysterious why that was ever spoken upon earth. From the sixth hour until the ninth hour there was darkness over the face of the earth. It was not the darkness of night, nor was it the darkness of an eclipse; it was nature's great expostulation and protest against the death and crucifixion of her Lord and Maker. This period of darkness from the sixth hour until the ninth hour was a period of silence. None of the Seven Words of the Cross were spoken during this time. But at the ninth hour Jesus broke the silence and pierced the darkness with His cry, "My God, why hast Thou forsaken me?"

What was behind that cry? Either Christ was mistaken or He was forsaken. If He was not forsaken, then He was mistaken, and we must conclude that the hours of suffering on the Cross had so weakened Him and distracted Him that His spirit temporarily collapsed, and He concluded that God had forsaken Him. Yet He was not really forsaken. He only thought that God had forgotten Him and forsaken Him.

But if Jesus was mistaken when He uttered this cry, then this is the only one of the utterances of Jesus which must be withdrawn. The thought that Jesus on the Cross was the victim of a misunderstanding and had a conviction of that which was not true can never be reconciled with the teaching of the Gospel that Jesus Christ was the Eternal Son of God.

But if Jesus was not mistaken in that cry, then He was actually forsaken of God. This experience marked the climax of His suffering for sin. This was the bitterness of the cup from which He asked to be delivered in the Garden of Gethsemane. Only Christ Himself had the right to ask such a question, for Christ was God's Eternal Son. The penalty upon sin is death, separation from God. This was the cup that Christ tasted for a moment on the Cross. With the burden of the world's sin upon Him He passed out into the lonely darkness. Only that experience can explain the strange shrinking of Christ from His death, and that agony and bloody sweat amid the shadows of Gethsemane when He cried, "If it be possible, let this cup pass from me!" That experience through which Christ passed on the Cross, and which wrung from His soul that amazed cry, "Why hast thou forsaken Me?" was the full price of redemption. It shows both the measure of God's wrath towards sin and the measure of God's love for man. On that cry rests the hope of our salvation. But because Christ asked it amid the darkness of the Cross, you and I need never ask that question or utter that cry of desolation.

> Yea once Immanuel's orphaned cry, His universe hath shaken—
> It went up single, echoless, My God, I am forsaken!
> It went up from His holy lips amid His lost creation,
> That of the lost no son should use those words of desolation.
> —Author Unknown

The Cross of Christ, that great mystery of divine wrath and justice and illimitable, immeasurable mercy and love, is the mystery that solves all other mysteries. When we survey the wondrous Cross on which the Prince of Glory died, we know that infinite love is at the heart of things, and that all things work together for good unto them that love God.

When God rejected the earnest, longing appeal of Moses, His servant, to enter the Land of Promise, and buried him there "by Nebo's lonely mountain," perhaps Moses wondered why. But when ages afterwards Moses and Elijah appeared in glory on the Mount of Transfiguration and spake together with Jesus concerning His approaching death on the Cross, I have no doubt that Moses felt satisfied with the ways of God.

> O lonely grave in Moab's land!
>   O dark Beth-Peor's hill!
> Speak to these curious hearts of ours,
>   And teach them to be still.
> God hath His mysteries of grace,
>   Ways that we cannot tell;
> He hides them deep, like the hidden sleep
>   Of him he loved so well.
>   —C. F. Alexander, "The Burial of Moses"

9

THE WEAKEST WORD

What is the weakest word? What is the word that is the weakest because it is the most useless? What is the word that men speak in sad reverie when they have let opportunity pass them by? What is the word men use when they have chosen a course of life and then are unhappy in that choice? What is the word that strikes the note of hopeless remorse and sorrow when men have made their bed and then find that they must lie upon it? What is the word that falls in distress from the lips of a mother as she stands over the still form of her dead child? What is the word men speak with accents of grief when they discover that while they slept in careless neglect those they love have been taken from them, and now their ears are sealed to all their passionate words of affection which waited too long for expression? What is the word that Joab put into the mouth of David when he was mourning over the death of Absalom? What is the word Balaam used when the angel of the Lord stopped him in his sinful path? What is the word the sisters at Bethany used when Christ came to see them? What is the word that is the short, true, but sad and hopeless epitaph on thousands of graves? What is the word that is cut over the portals of the city of the lost? That word is *if* (2 Samuel 19:6).

If is the weakest word because it is the most useless. What did an if ever do for God or man? If breaks no chains of evil habit, mends no flaws in men's characters. If never brings back a lost opportunity and never opens a door that neglect or sin has closed. If never brings back a day that has been lost. If never armed one for the battle of life. If never preached a sermon, wrote a book, built a house, invented an engine, plowed a field, or conquered a city. If never opened the doors of death and brought back the life that was gone. If never turned a soul to repentance towards God and faith in the Lord Jesus Christ.

David's If

"If Absalom had lived." This was an if which was spoken by Joab. But in reality it is an if which that stern captain of the host put into the mouth of David. It was spoken by Joab at the conclusion of one of the most moving scenes in the Bible, or out of it. As the troops marched out that morning to battle in the Woods of Ephraim against Absalom's rebel host, David charged each of his captains, Ittai, Abishai, and Joab, as they marched by with their veteran divisions, to deal gently with Absalom. Full of affection for his blackguard son, David is fearfullest he should be slain in the battle. "Deal gently for my sake with the young man, even with Absalom." But when Joab saw Absalom hanging there under the oak, caught by the luxurious hair of which he was so proud, he thought more of the safety of the kingdom than he did of David's sorrow, and taking three darts he thrust them through the heart of the hapless Absalom.

All through the hours of the long day, when the battle was raging, David sat between the gates of the city, waiting for tidings, while the watchman on the roof over the gate kept a lookout for runners who would bring news of the battle. At length Ahimaaz was discerned approaching the city. "When David learned who it was, his heart was full of hope, for, he said, "He is a good man and cometh with good tidings." But Ahimaaz had not learned all that had happened in that Wood of Ephraim. All he knew was that the army of Absalom had been defeated, and when David said to him, "Is the young man Absalom safe," all Ahimaaz could answer was, "I saw a great tumult, but I knew not what it was." David told him to turn aside while he waited for the coming of the second runner.

This runner, Cushi, knew that Absalom had been slain. When David said to him, "Is the young man Absalom safe?" Cushi replied, "The enemies of my lord the King, and all that rise up against thee to do thee hurt, be as that young man is." When he heard that, David threw his mantle over his head and went up to the chamber over the gate to weep alone, and as he went thus he said, "O my son Absalom! my son, my son Absalom! would God I had died for thee! O Absalom, my son, my son!"

Poor David! The sorrow that had overwhelmed him had banished all thought of his kingdom and his power and prestige as a ruler. Like Othello he felt that his occupation was gone.

> O now forever,
> Farewell the tranquil mind! Farewell, content.
> Farewell the plumed troop and the big wars
> That make ambition virtue! O farewell!
> Farewell the neighing steed and the shrill trump
> The spirit-stirring drum, the ear-piercing fife,
> The royal banner and all quality,
> Pride, pomp, and circumstance of glorious war.
> —Shakespeare, *Othello*

Joab, hard-hearted, but practical and useful man, was displeased at David's intemperate grief, and told him that in his unrestrained mourning for Absalom he had forgotten the brave men who fought and died for him on the field of battle that he might be restored to the throne. "For I perceive," said Joab, "that if Absalom had lived, then it had pleased thee well." Brought to himself by Joab's gruff but sensible remark, and timely, too, David composed himself, came out of the chamber where he was mourning, and took his royal seat at the gate of the city where all his army could see him and salute him.

Intemperate sorrow, until corrected by Joab, unfitted David for his great responsibilities as a king. The fact is that David, giving himself over to his grief, was thinking of life as it might have been, and of the Kingdom as it might have been, if Absalom had lived. That, Joab correctly discerned, was the present principle of David's life. In that sublime and touching

lament, "O Absalom, my son, would God I had died for thee!"
you can read also the cadence of his sorrowful thought, "If
Absalom had only lived," "If he had not been slain in the midst
of the battle." But it was a vain and useless if. Absalom was
dead. David's sorrow could not bring him hack. All that his
unrestrained grief now did was to unfit him for his work as a
king.

That pitiful if of David has been echoed and re-echoed by
many a sorrowing and bereaved soul. We would not speak
carelessly or lightly of the deep sorrow that has come to any
grieving heart here tonight, but your effort to reconstruct the
present, to think always of how life might be now if the loved
one had not been taken by death, is altogether futile, unset-
tling, and distracting. No plaintive if can alter the decree of
God. The thing to do is to do what Joab persuaded the mourning David to do, "Conquer your sorrow and take up the duties
of life." Joab rightly told David that his sorrow was selfish, in
that his indulgence in it kept him from performing the duty
which he owed to his subjects. We all have a duty to perform
in the world and towards those who are about us, but that duty
cannot be performed if we give ourselves over to unmeasured
grief and pronounce today and tomorrow and tomorrow that
weakest and most useless of all words, if.

BALAAM'S IF

Balaam is one of the most gifted, interesting, fascinating,
and tragic personalities of the Old Testament. He lived afar
off in the country along the Euphrates River, and so great was
his reputation as a prophet and diviner, that when Balak, King
of Moab, heard that the Israelites were approaching his bor-
ders, he dispatched messengers to Balaam asking him to come
and curse the invaders.

When the ambassadors appeared at his home and offered
him great rewards if he would go with them and curse Israel,
Balaam invited them to spend the night while he inquired of
the Lord. In the night the message came to him, "Thou shalt
not go with them; thou shalt not curse the people, for they are
blessed." But the king of Noah, Balak, going on the principle

that every man has a price, sent yet again princes, more and more honorable. This second time Balaam boastfully answered them, "If Balak would give me his house full of silver and gold, I cannot go beyond the word of the Lord my God, to do less or more." But this boast was followed by a dangerous invitation. He invited the messengers to spend a second night with him, to see what the Lord might say more unto him. He evidently hoped that the Lord would change his mind. In the night Balaam seemed to get the consent for which he had been seeking, and in the morning he saddled his ass and in eager haste set off with the princes of Moab.

But God's anger was kindled against him because he went. Where the path led between two walls by a vineyard, Balaam's beast suddenly frightened, and in trying to get away bruised the prophet's foot against the wall, whereupon Balaam took to beating his ass. Then the cause of the animal's fright was disclosed to Balaam. The angel of the Lord was standing in the path with drawn sword in his hand. When Balaam saw the angel he was frightened and said, "I have sinned for I knew not that thou stoodest in the way against me. Now, therefore, if it displease thee, I will get me back again." But the angel of the Lord said, "Go with the men!"

Balaam's if was the weak if of a man who tries to serve two masters. He desired to share the destiny of the people of God, but at the same time he wanted the rewards for cursing Israel. He prayed, "Let me die the death of the righteous, and let my last end be like his." Yet he died in disgrace, fighting in the ranks among the enemies of Israel. He was quite willing to be righteous, if it did not cost too much, if it did not involve too much of a surrender of this world's goods.

In that respect Balaam has many successors. There is always an if attached to their religious faith and conviction. They seek the Lord, but not with their whole hearts. In *Pilgrim's Progress* John Bunyan tells how Christian saw a beautiful palace on a hill. Around the door stood a great company of men desirous to go in, but who dared not make the effort. At a tableside near the door there sat a man with a book and an ink horn, ready to put down the name of him who would enter into the palace. In the doorway stood men in armor, ready to hold back and wound anyone who attempted to enter. All who stood about were starting back with fear, when Christian saw a man of stout countenance go up to the one who had the inkhorn and say to him, "Set my name down, Sir!" Then he put his helmet over his head, drew his sword, and rushed upon the armed men who guarded the door of the palace. After receiving and giving many wounds he cut his way into the palace, where were heard voices of those who walked in gold raiment on the top of the palace, saying,

> Come, Come in!
> Eternal glory thou shalt win.

It is not enough to wish for a godly life; we must fight for it. It is not enough to desire to go to heaven; we reach heaven through peril, toil, and pain.

The if of Balaam was the weak if of a man who starts on an evil course with the reservation in his mind that if it proves to be too difficult or dangerous he will turn back. When Balaam saw the angel with the drawn sword in his hand, he said to the angel, "I have sinned, for I knew not that thou stoodest in the way against me. Now, therefore, if it displease thee, I will get me back again." Balaam thought he could turn back whenever he wanted to, but the angel tells him he must go on. He speaks as if he does not really know that what he has done is displeasing to God, and tells God that if it is wrong he will go back. That if shows there was no real contrition and no real repentance on the part of Balaam. He was somewhat afraid of the possible consequences of his sin, but had no true sense of sin. When we stand before God there is no if as to our condition and our great need. What is fitting and appropriate for all of us is not, "If it displease thee," but, "God be merciful to me the chief of sinners."

Men who set out on an evil path with the thought in mind that one day they will turn back if that path proves dangerous and difficult are sadly deluded. When the swords of judgment begin to flash, then they say that they will turn and go back. But often, as in the case of Balaam, they have gone too far to turn back. Accumulation of habit, repeated indulgence of desire, repeated disobedience of God's Word—all this says to them, like the angel of judgment whose sword flashed before the face of the frightened prophet on the way to Noah, "Go on! Now you cannot go back! Go with the men!"

MARY AND MARTHA'S IF

In some village beyond the Jordan the word was brought to Jesus that Lazarus, whom He loved, was sick. Mary and Martha, the sisters of Lazarus, were sure that as soon as Jesus heard that it was Lazarus who was sick He would start for Bethany. But instead of doing that, Jesus remained two days where He was. You can imagine Mary or Martha taking their stand by the roadside and looking down the highway in the direction of Jericho from which Jesus would come. But two days passed and Jesus had not come, and while He was absent, death came. Lazarus was dead. When He learned that Lazarus was dead, Jesus at length started for Bethany. As He drew near to the village, four days after the death and the burial of Lazarus, He was met on the outskirts of the town, first of all, by Martha, who had hurried out to meet Him as soon as she heard that He was coming. When she saw Jesus, Martha said, "Lord, if Thou hadst been here, our brother had not died." Then Mary, too, came, and falling at the feet of Jesus, repeated the saying of Martha, "Lord, if Thou hadst been here, my brother had not died."

There was a note of almost reproach in the plaintive words of Martha and Mary, as if they had said, "Lord, if Thou hadst come when we first sent for thee, Thou wouldst have been able to save Lazarus from the grave." Although a natural one, it was a weak if, because it was an attempt to reconstruct and change the past. It was God's will that Lazarus should die, and as it turned out, be raised again from the dead for the conversion of sinners and the glory of God. To attach any if to the decrees of God is both futile and unworthy. Instead of saying, "If it had been otherwise with me," "If the appointment of fate had been different," we ought to say, "What is it that God has in mind in what He has appointed? What great purpose is there in His providence for me?"

How often we come across persons who are trying to relive and reconstruct their life upon an if. Often I have heard bereaved and mourning friends say practically what Mary and Martha said; that if some circumstance had been different their loved one would not have died. "If I had called the doctor sooner," or "If I had called another doctor," or "If I had taken him to the hospital." Thus they burden themselves and sadden their life by an impossible presupposition; namely, that if they had done something a little different, or someone else had done something a little different, God's decree would have been changed, and life today would have been altogether different for them. But this is an impossible hypothesis. What is has been appointed. What we have written we have written, and there are no mistakes in the grand eternal plan of God.

Instead of looking back and thinking of what might have been, let us accept what is, look forward, and plan and aim at greater things in the future. Let us not weakly seek to rebuild the past, for that is always an impossible task, but let us live in the present and dedicate ourselves to the future, and always let us be confident of this, as those two mourning sisters discovered after their crushing sorrow, that God never leaves us and never forsakes us, and that always His everlasting arms are around us and about us. To God's love in Christ there is no if.

10

THE WORD THAT OPENS HEAVEN

What is the word that opens heaven? What is the word that no one can pronounce without the Holy Spirit? What is the word that brings a sinner back from the far country to his father's house? What is the word that guardian angels like to hear on our lips? What is the word which when pronounced by man strikes an immediate chord of answering joy in heaven? What is the word that Job used after God answered him out of the whirlwind?

What is the word with which Jesus began to preach? What is the word with which Peter addressed the multitudes on the day of Pentecost? What is the word that David spoke when the prophet Nathan rebuked him for his hideous transgression? What is the word that Manasseli, the aged and wicked king of Judah, spoke in captivity? What is the word that Peter uttered when he went out into the night and wept bitterly? What is the word that opened the gates of Paradise to the dying thief? What is the word which is timely and appropriate on the lips of the ripened saint, as well as on the lips of the most hardened sinner? What is the word which cannot be spoken in hell, and which no one in heaven ever needs to use? That word is *repent!* "Except ye repent"—Luke 13:3.

Repentance is a word which rings through every part of the Bible, from beginning to end. It was the burden of the preaching of the prophets, the apostles, and of Christ Himself. Repentance sums up the Gospel, for after He had risen from the dead Christ told His disciples to go forth and preach repentance and the remission of sins through His name. Repentance is the word that opens heaven, for only a forgiven sinner can enter heaven, and only a sinner who repents can be forgiven.

The examples of repentance illuminate the pages of the Bible. They afford us the Bible's most moving and inspiring scenes. When we tell the story of the men who repented we have proclaimed the full and glorious Gospel of the blessed God. If in the case of any of the words chosen thus far there has been any doubt in your mind as to whether or not the choice is justified and proven by the Scriptures, certainly there will be no doubt or question as to whether or not the Bible in every part of it illustrates and proves that repentance is the word that opens heaven. Indeed, the instances of repentance are so numerous and so beautiful that one hardly knows which stories of repentance to choose.

AN OLD MAN'S REPENTANCE

We don't talk much about old people today. Every one tries to disguise the fact that he is old, or is getting old. The whole emphasis of popular preaching and popular literature is upon youth, and no doubt, to a very over-balanced degree. But the fact is that there are a lot of old people in the world, and they ought not to be passed over or forgotten. Their souls are of the same value in the sight of God as the soul of a boy, or the soul of a youth in his teens. There is another striking and very solemn fact, too, about old men, and that is that if they have not repented before they grew old they hardly ever repent. Therefore, the story of repentance which I shall now tell you is all the more remarkable.

Manasseh is the prodigal son of the Old Testament. He had for a father one of the godliest men in the Bible, Hezekiah, and no doubt a godly mother. He ascended the throne when he was twelve years of age, at the death of his father. His reign was a long nightmare of wickedness, idolatry, and cruelty. He reared altars for Baal, and made groves and worshipped all the host of heaven. The climax to his idolatry was his building altars to the heathen gods in the very temple of Jehovah, where he set up a carved image. He caused his children to pass through the fire and dealt with witches and wizards. In addition to all this he shed innocent blood. Among the victims of his persecution, according to a very ancient tradition, was the prophet Isaiah, whom Manasseh sawed asunder, because the prophet had rebuked him for his sins. The sacred chronicler says of Manasseh that "he made the people of Israel worse than the heathen themselves."

In the noontime of his wicked prosperity Manasseh was captured by the cruel Assyrians, who mutilated him, put him in an iron cage, and carried him a prisoner to Babylon. There Manasseh, softened by his sufferings, repented of his sins and called upon God. When he had been restored to the throne of Jerusalem he devoted the strength and energy left to him in the remaining years of his reign to undo the great evil that he had done to Israel. With sorrow and contrition he threw away the strange gods, repaired the altar of God, and did what he could to persuade the nation, which he had before seduced, to turn again and follow the true God.

Manasseh sinned against a godly training, and as the son of a godly father, became a monster of unbelief. Now and then you see that, and if you have listened to the bitterness of such an unbeliever, you realize all the more how wonderful was the repentance of Manasseh. Suffering and hardship and pain sometimes only intensify man's rebellion to God. But if accepted in humility, it can turn man back to God. That was what happened in the case of Manasseh. Scoff at a deathbed repentance, if you will, and certainly this was almost a deathbed repentance, for Manasseh brought to God only the dregs of his life. Yet for that reason, Manasseh's repentance is all the more memorable. After a half century in sin, Manasseh returns to God. Thank God, no one is ever too far gone, too hardened in his transgression, to repent. To the youth who has turned from God and to the old man also are spoken those words of hope and mercy, "Let the wicked forsake his way, the unrighteous man his thought, and let him return unto the Lord for he will have mercy, and unto our God for He will abundantly pardon."

DAVID'S REPENTANCE

Whoever is left out in the list of great penitents in the Bible, one must not omit David, the greatest sinner and the greatest saint of the Old Testament. Enemies of God have always scoffed at David and the high title with which his name is associated in the Bible, David, "the man after God's heart." They have fixed upon David's terrible fall and his heinous transgression, and have held him up as an example of the illustrious worthies of the Old Testament and have said that if such men were around today they would be in the penitentiary or hung from the gallows.

But a Christian man who knows his own heart, and who knows that the heart is desperately wicked and deceitful above all else, will never be troubled by the fall of David. On the contrary, he will rejoice that the Bible records this dark chapter in David's life. If David had not fallen so low, his repentance would not have been so wonderful, and so blessed of God, for all the generations of men. In his penitential prayer, David prayed, "Restore unto me the joy of thy salvation, and then shall I teach transgressors thy ways." Yes, that is what David has been doing through the ages, teaching men the deceitfulness and sinfulness of their own hearts, and also the wonderful mercy of God, and that David will do unto the remotest generation.

I think that Nathan is almost the most courageous preacher and the most tender preacher of whom we have any record. Every preacher ought to be courageous in declaring the will of God, yet tender in seeking to reclaim the sinner. The human heart is the same from age to age, and there is nothing new or old in David's sin. He fell in love with a beautiful woman who happened to be the wife of another man. Although he was King, and according to the customs of the age might have done as he pleased, David tried to cover up his crime by the murder of the woman's husband. He sent him into the forefront of the hottest battle with orders to his commanding officer to retire from him so that he would fall fighting the foe. But it was just the same as if David had slain him with his own hand. This, indeed, was the worst sin. The cruel and cowardly and treacherous murder of Uriah was another, and sometimes from the standpoint of the sinner, seems to make necessary a second transgression, which is always worse than the first.

God waited for David to repent. The extraordinary thing is that David, so schooled in the thought of God, and naturally a man of such deep religious feeling, could have gone through these terrible transgressions and his conscience not have constantly pierced him and rebuked him. But apparently it did not, and that fact reveals to us the strange blindness that sin casts over the sinner. He can see the presence and the heinousness of sin in other men, but not in himself. In every story of a breakdown like that of David it will be found that the very sin in which the man was indulging dulled and blunted his sensibilities. "Who can understand his errors? Cleanse thou me from secret faults."

God waited long for David to repent, and then he sent the prophet Nathan. With masterly skill and exquisite tenderness Nathan told David the story of the cruel rich man who had numerous flocks and herds, and yet who, when a guest came to visit him, took the poor man's pet lamb and slew it for the table of his guest. When he heard this tale of almost unbelievable hardness of heart, David reached for his sword, saying, "Bring that man before me! As the Lord liveth, he shall surely die!" Then Nathan drew his sword and thrust it home with the words, "Thou art the man!" With riches and wives and honors, David had taken the wife of a poor soldier in his army to gratify his passions. "Thou art the man!"

If Nathan had talked that way with any other king but David, his head would have come off. But David repented and said, "I have sinned." There was no doubt, either, about the sincerity of his repentance, for immediately the prophet answered, "The Lord hath put away thy sin." Yet, forgiven though he was, David had to bear the temporal penalties of his sin. There is nothing strange about that, either. A man can sin for years against his body and against his mind, and if he turns and repents, he is forgiven, but the God who forgives him does not cancel the law of retribution in the man's own body, for "whatsoever a man soweth that shall he also reap." Nathan told David that because his sin would cause the enemies of God to scoff and rejoice, the sword would never depart from his house. It never did. Time and again we see the flashing of that sword of judgment: in the vile conduct and incest of Amnon, in the murder of Amnon by Absalom, in the rebellion of Absalom, in the death of Absalom in the Wood of Ephraim, and all the sorrow and suffering of David reaching its tremendous climax in that pathetic lamentation, "O Absalom, my son, would God I had died for thee!"

Yes, David had to suffer, but he suffered as a forgiven man. The joy of salvation had been restored to David. His repentance had opened for him once more the gates of heaven. If any man has sinned like David, there is only one path that will bring him back to self respect and communion with God, and that is the path of repentance.

The great music of heaven will be furnished, not by the unfallen angels, although that will be grand and glorious music, but by penitent and forgiven sinners. I fancied that, as in a dream, I was in heaven, and trod the streets of the New Jerusalem. I listened, spellbound and enthralled, to the great music of heaven, the ten thousand times ten thousand on the sea of glass mingled with fire, and harpers playing their harps. But suddenly there was silence in heaven for the space of half an hour. The harps were tuneless, the trumpets mute, and the voice of the ten thousand times ten thousand was hushed. Then near the throne I saw a harper take up his harp, and as he smote his harp he also sang. The music was of heaven, and yet I thought I heard in it the strains of earth also. I thought I discerned in the music of this harper and his singing the melody that can come only out of the experience of temptation and suffering and sin forgiven. While he played and sang, all others were silent. I turned to one of the heavenly throng and said to him, "Who is this singer? And why are all the others silent and attentive?" He answered, "They are silent and their harps unsmitten because they are listening to the music of David, the sweet singer of Israel, and the sweetest singer of heaven, the greatest sinner and the greatest saint of the Bible."

After listening to the great music of David in heaven, we can hardly now come back to earth and speak of others whose repentance opened for them the gate of heaven. Time would fail to tell of St. Paul, who in a moment turned from being the greatest enemy of Christ to become his greatest friend; of that "woman who was a sinner," who washed the Savior's feet with the tears of repentance and love and wiped them with the hair of her head; of Peter, who, when he had cursed and denied his Master, was called to himself by the look of love when Jesus turned and looked upon him, and went out into the night to weep bitterly those tears of repentance that washed his soul and brought him back to Christ; and of that poor thief who hung at the Redeemer's side on the Cross, and who, while his companion mocked and cursed, repented of his sin and asked Jesus to remember him, and to whom Jesus immediately opened the gate of Heaven and said, "Today shalt thou be with Me in Paradise!"

Wonderful music all these repentant sinners have given to the Church on earth and to the Church in Heaven. Wonderful light and beauty they have shed upon the pages of Scripture. Wonderful trophies they are to the saving and cleansing and redeeming power of the Blood of Christ. May their music reach tonight some soul who has sinned against God and turn his feet heavenward, where a father's welcome awaits him; the same welcome that awaited that penitent of whom Jesus told in the great parable of repentance, the son who repented in the far country and said, "I have sinned against heaven and in thy sight"; and whom, when he came back, his father saw a great way off, and ran and fell on his neck and kissed him. That same welcome awaits every soul that repents. The best robe is ready, and ready the golden ring of reconciliation, and the angels, too, are ready to strike again their harps and rejoice over one sinner that repenteth.

11

THE WORD THAT TAKES IN ALL OTHERS

What is the word that takes in all other words? One thought that it was Savior; another, whosoever; and others, God, Jesus, eternity; the greater number voted for love. But none of these is the word that takes in all others.

What is that word? What is the word that expresses God's sublime thought for man ever since He said, "Let us make man in our image"? What is the word that fulfills the hope and promise of all other words? What is the word that consummates the redemptive labors of Christ? What is the word that cancels the woe of this life and dries all tears? What is the word that makes all things new? What is the word before which sorrow and sighing flee away? What is the word that Jacob saw in letters of gold when he dreamed his dream at Bethel, that Stephen saw written across the sky when he was dying, that John saw written in rainbow colors across the sky at Patmos? What is the word that awakens every chord in the breast of man to sweet vibration? What is the word that is God's word for home? That word is *heaven*. "I saw and behold a door open in heaven"—Revelation 4:1.

Yes, here is the word that takes in all other words. Is there any noble thought of the mind that it does not measure? Is there any holy longing of the soul that it does not satisfy? Is there any grand purpose of God that it leaves out? Is there any work of Satan that it does not overthrow? Is there any wound that it does not heal? Has earth any sorrow that heaven cannot quench? Is there any dream of man's spirit that heaven does not make a beautiful reality? Is there any chord in man's heart that heaven does not strike? No, heaven is the word that takes in all others, fulfilling them, transforming them, transfiguring them, and illuminating them. It is the lost chord which, struck by the pierced hand of Christ, awakens all the music of time and of eternity!

In speaking of the other great words in the Bible and in human speech, with each word we tried to prove and illustrate our proposition, not by abstract reasoning, but by illustration from the experience of men and women in the Bible. But can we do this in the case of this word, heaven? At first it would not seem to be possible, for, however great and beautiful heaven may be, no one has ever come back to tell us what it is like. There is no earthly and mortal experience or reality which cannot be illustrated by the men and women of the Bible, but heaven is not a mortal or earthly experience. That is so, but the Bible is a wonderful book, and I think we can learn and desire a great deal about heaven from the history and experience of some of the men who appear in the pages of the Bible, men to whom heaven was opened for a moment to view, and who, for a brief moment at least, had the experience of the heavenly life.

JACOB AT THE GATE OF HEAVEN

A traveler is coming along the desert highway. All that one sees is bleak stretches of country, with here and there gaunt, naked yellow hills. To the west, the tops of the mountains are rapidly sinking into shadow as the draperies of night fall about their shoulders.

The solitary traveler is a young man in the vigor of life, but when he comes to a standstill we can see that in his face there are signs not only of physical weariness and fatigue, but also of dejection and fatigue of spirit. There is a look also of fear and of dread and guilt, for the man has sinned greatly and deeply. What a difference sin makes in life! Only a few days ago this youth was the favored son in a happy home, with care, comfort, and plenty. Tonight he is a lonely fugitive, weary, conscience smitten, and afraid. Sin had driven him out. That is what sin is always doing, driving man out, separating him from companionship, from happiness and peace of spirit.

Warned by the approach of night, Jacob looks about for a place where he can sleep. He selects a spot somewhat sheltered from the wind, and where a flat stone will serve as a pillow. He lifts his wallet from his shoulder, and putting his staff by his side, draws his mantle over his head, lest the moon should smite him by night. Soon he is in the deep, deep sleep of physical fatigue and heart sorrow.

But as he sleeps, lo, he dreams. In his dream he sees a ladder set up on the earth, and the top of it reaches to heaven, and behold, the angels of God ascending and descending on it. At the top of the ladder was the Lord God, Who said to Jacob, "I am the Lord God of Abraham thy father. The land whereon thy liest, to thee will I give it and to thy seed. Behold, I am with thee, and will keep thee in all places wherever thou goest and will bring thee again into this land."

When Jacob awoke out of his slumber, with that wonderful dream still fresh in his mind, he said, "Surely, the Lord is in this place, and I knew it not. How dreadful is this place! This is none other than the house of God, and this is the gate of heaven." Jacob then set up the stone on which he had slept as a pillar, and pouring oil upon it, vowed that he would come there and worship when God brought him back to his father's land and his father's house.

That is what we all need on our earthly journey and pilgrimage, a dream and a vision like that, a bit and a glimpse of heaven in the very midst of our earthly life. We want a light to shine out of heaven, and the angels to come down and tell us that we are not alone, that God is with us and His love is around us wherever we go.

ST. PAUL IN HEAVEN

Early in his Christian ministry, the Apostle Paul had an experience of heaven, and this is what he says about it: "I knew a man in Christ about fourteen years ago. (Whether in the body I cannot tell, or whether out of the body I cannot tell; God knoweth.) Such a one caught up to the third heaven, and I knew such a man (whether in the body or out of the body, God knoweth). How he was caught up into paradise and heard unspeakable words which are not lawful for a man to utter. Of such a one will I glory."

By this Paul means that he glories in the recollection of that heavenly experience, for it came to him as a vindication, a confirmation of his claims as a Christian apostle. We regret, of course, that St. Paul did not relate his experiences. The reason he gives is that it is not lawful for him to utter what he had heard and seen there. That must mean that it is not possible to translate into the speech of this world what he heard and saw and felt when he was in heaven. Yet I sometimes wonder if that magnificent account of the heavenly life which he gives in the First Letter to the Corinthians, where he describes the spiritual body of the Resurrection, when the mortal has put on immortality and the corruptible has put on incorruption and death is swallowed up in victory, was not based upon this great experience that he had when he was caught up into the third heaven. Also that other passage in his Second Letter, where he says that we have a building of God, a house not made with hands, eternal in the heavens, and that we earnestly desire to be clothed upon with our house which is in heaven—if that, too, is not in some way a reflection of what he heard and saw in this visit to heaven. But suffice it for us to know that Paul had an actual experience of the heavenly world. He talks of it as one who has been there, and was overwhelmed by the beauty and splendor of it.

Many years ago a young Presbyterian minister, and a member of the famous Tennent family, fell into a trance. By every test he seemed to have expired, and the day for his funeral had been appointed. But when the friends had assembled he showed signs of life, and in due time was resuscitated. In his record of the trance he said that he found himself in the heavenly world under the conduct of a heavenly guide. There he beheld ineffable glory and an innumerable company of happy beings. Thrilled with their great joy, he besought his heavenly conductor to permit him to join them. But to his great sorrow his guide told him that he must return to earth and be a witness of what he had seen.

It is quite conceivable that for the purposes of his grace God should grant to men a fleeting vision of heaven's splendors. Although this has not been granted, save in a few authentic instances like that of St. Paul, the Scriptures say enough about the heavenly life to let us know that it will be a life of splendor and of power, of peace and of beauty. Marco Polo was the great Venetian traveler and explorer who went to the far east in the thirteenth century. When he was dying he was urged by some of those who stood about him to recant and withdraw the tales he had told about the wonders of China and the lands of the Far East. But his reply was, "I have not told half of what I saw." Whatever heaven is, and wherever it is, this much is certain, we shall never be able to tell the hundredth cart of what it is like.

Perhaps one of the most luminous statements of St. Paul on the subject is, that as we have borne the image of the earthly we shall bear the image of the heavenly. This means that we have a nature and image appropriate to our life here on earth, and that in the life to come in heaven we shall have a nature, a body, and a spirit appropriate to the heavenly life. What will the "image of the heavenly" be in that life which is to come?

The image of the heavenly will be the image of power and of strength. Too often in this world our body is that part of us which hinders us from doing good. It is a prison for the spirit, rather than its ally and associate. But there we shall go from strength to strength. The body which death sows in weakness will be raised in power.

The image of the heavenly will be the image of great and noble achievement. To be good, and to do good, and to make others good, is the highest of all tasks. When you open the pages of the Apocalypse you hear the rumble and stir of great events. Certainly heaven will not be just an endless singing school, but an arena of boundless energy. What has mighty St. Paul been doing all these ages since he was beheaded at the Pyramid of Caestius near the gates of Rome? What has St.

John been doing all these years since he wrote the words, "When he shall appear we shall be like him"?

Again, the image of the heavenly will be the image of the holy and sinless. Here sin reigneth, and everywhere is the shadow of its curse. Every day you must fight against sin in your own life. But in heaven there shall be no more curse and no more sin.

The image of the heavenly will be the image of great joy. Man was made for joy. The morning stars sang together, and all the sons of God shouted for joy when man was created. The deepest pathos of life in this world is the fact of man's longing for joy and happiness and his capacity for it, and yet the fullest joy and happiness escape him. But there eternal joy shall reign. At thy right hand there is fullness of joy. I have no doubt that one of the highest joys of heaven will be the joy of fellowship and reunion with those whom we knew and loved in this world.

> The eternal form shall still divide,
> The eternal soul from all beside,
> And I shall know him when we meet.
> —Author Unknown

When Paul told the mourning Christians at Thessalonica that they were not to mourn as those who had no hope, because the dead in Christ shall rise first, that can only mean that they were to have the great joy and comfort of reunion with the believing dead.

> It is an old belief
> That on some solemn shore,
> Beyond the sphere of grief,
> Dear friends shall meet once more.
>
> Beyond the sphere of time,
> And sin, and fate's control,
> Serene in changeless prime
> Of body and of soul.

That creed I fain would keep,
This hope I'll not forego;
Eternal be the sleep?
If not to waken so.

—Author Unknown

THE THIEF IN HEAVEN

Their is another man in the Bible who, we are sure, went to heaven upon the direct invitation and promise of Christ. When the Dying Thief, after he had rebuked his fellow thief for his unbelief and blasphemy, turned to Jesus and said, "Jesus, remember me when Thou comest in Thy Kingdom." Jesus answered, "Today shalt thou be with Me in Paradise."

I was thinking once of heaven and the heavenly life when lo, as if in answer to my thought and desire—for heaven belongs unto those who think about it—the Penitent Thief stood before me. He was much as I had pictured him, and yet something unearthly and supernal, too: a brightness of glory, a look of immeasurable strength, and also of infinite peace. As he seemed to wait for me to speak, I said: "Penitent Thief, I have thought much and spoken much, and written much of the life to come, yet you are the only one I have ever met who has really been in heaven. Tell me, then, thief, is there indeed a life to come? For the longer I live and the more I think about it, the more I come to that everything great and good in this life depends upon the fact of the life to come."

Is there truth in life eternal?
   Will our memories never die?
Shall we relive in realms supernal
   Life's resplendent and glorious lie?
Death has not one shape so frightful
   But defiantly I would brave it.
Earth has nothing so delightful
   But my soul would scorne to crave it,
   Could I know for sure, for certain,
   That the falling of the curtain,
   And the folding of the hands

Is the full and final casting
Of accounts for the everlasting!
Everlasting and everlasting!"

—Author Unknown

"Yes, Mortal, there is a life to come, and I by your side am the proof of it."

"But, Thief—it will not offend you if I call you by that name?"

"No, forever in heaven I am known as the Penitent Thief."

"Well, Thief, tell me more of heaven. There is no more sin, and pain and sorrow and death there?"

"No, these are all the former things which as St. John said, have passed away."

"And the body? Is this the same body, Dying Thief, that was pierced on the Cross?"

"Yes. But changed now into the Spiritual Body. Once I bore the image of the earth; now I bear the image of the heavenly."

"Tell me, then, Thief, of the life, the occupations in heaven? What labors are performed there?"

"Vast is God's universe, and for all in heaven there is a noble work to do."

"And for thee?"

"Work like this, to encourage faith, to persuade sinners to repent."

"What else?"

"The social joys, the society of the good and the great and the believing of all the ages. Although only a poor thief, I was received into the company of Abraham and Elijah and Isaiah and David, and all those who came after me into heaven—Peter, John, and Paul."

"And our friends and loved ones, Thief? Shall we meet them and know them there? Is that heavenly life too high and too pure for memory?"

"Ah, no; memory remains. It is one of heaven's highest joys. There friend shall meet with friend, and life's broken and interrupted companionship shall be resumed, never again to be broken. They shall go no more out and come no more in."

"And what is best of all there, Thief? Sum it all up for me, if you can, in a single word."

"The best of all is Jesus. To be in heaven is to be with Him. That is what He told me in that dark and fearful hour on the Cross—'Today shalt thou be with Me in Paradise.' I can tell you nothing more wonderful about heaven than that. You will be with Christ."

"And by how many gates may we enter heaven, Thief?"

"By one only, the gate of repentance, the gate by which I entered—there is no other way. Now go back to that heavenly world, to its beautiful lights, its ravishing music, its noble labor and undertaking, and its pleasures evermore at the right hand of God."

"Thou hast made heaven very real to me. Farewell, Thief, till we meet again. And if to the redeemed in heaven it is permitted to pray for the souls of men on earth, then, Thief, remember me at the throne of God, and ask the Savior who remembered thee on the cross to remember me, and all those to whom I preach tonight. Farewell!"

12

THE SWEETEST AND BITTEREST WORD

How can a word he both sweet and bitter? Ah, that is one of the mysteries of life, one of the mysteries of the human heart. The same question was asked a long time ago by St. James, "Doth a fountain send forth at the same time sweet waters and bitter?" No, no fountain ever did that, but the fountain of the human heart does, and therefore there is a word that is both the sweetest and bitterest word that the tongue can pronounce.

What is that word? What is the word that is a strong argument for the existence of the soul, of God, and of the hereafter? What is the word that is the well-stored library of the mind? What is the word that is the rich treasury of life? What is the word that makes the joys of childhood to live again? What is the word that "oft in the stilly night" brings the light of other days around us? What is the word that recreates the fond ambitions and hopes of youth? What is the word that restores the blessedness that once we knew when first we saw the Lord?

What is the word that rekindles the fires of affection and reunites hearts once separated by death? What is the word which is so swift in its movement, that compared with it the tempest itself lags behind and the swift winged arrows of light? What is the word before whose magic touch time retreats and

space is non-existent? What is the word which gives us a kingdom where moth doth not corrupt nor thieves break through
and steal? What is the word which is a companion which never
deserts us when riches take wings, when reputation sees, when
adversity's chill winds begin to blow? What is the word that is
the angel with the backward look? What is the word that cheers
the sleepless bed and companions us in the silent watches of
the night?

And what is that same word that makes sin a fact, and hell a
reasonable and dreaded probability; that burns the tongue which
pronounces it; that makes dreadful the sleepless hours of the
night; that clouds the brightest day, poisons the sweetest flower,
and turns the softest music into discord? What is the word
that cannot be bought for a bribe, entreated or persuaded?
What is the word that rises like a ghost at the banquet of joy;
that lays a restraining arm on him who would battle for the
good? What is the word that invades the most carefully guarded
palace, and picks the most intricate lock of defense? What is
the word that is the soul's judge and jailer? What is the word
that keeps the soul from returning to lost gardens of peace and
happiness, as the angel with his flaming sword, turning every
way, kept the way of the Tree of Life?

That word is *memory*. "Son, Remember"—Luke 16:25. "O
memories that bless and burn!"

In his gripping tale, "The Haunted Man," Charles Dickens
tells of a chemist who sat before the fire, troubled with unhappy memories. As he sat there in dismal reverie, a phantom
appeared and offered the haunted man the opportunity to have
his memory destroyed. He immediately closed with the offer,
and henceforth was a man not only without any memory, but
had the dread power to strip other men of their memories. But
the gift was a disappointment. So great was his misery, and so
great the misery that he had inflicted upon others, that he
besought the phantom to restore to him his memory. The tale
comes to a conclusion with the man's grateful and earnest
prayer, "Lord, keep my memory green."

I suppose that story tells the truth. Without memory, man
would not be man, and perhaps if one had to choose between
keeping his memory, although it had many bitter things in it,

and having no memory at all, he would probably choose the former state. But that in no way invalidates the proposition of this sermon, that memory is the sweetest and the bitterest word.

MEMORY AS THE SWEETEST WORD

The English philosopher John Locke once wrote that "memory is the only heaven out of which a man cannot be cast." By the magic of memory all the treasures of the past are ours. James Barrie said that God gave us memory that we might have roses in December. Here again we draw upon that inexhaustible storehouse, the biographies of men in the Bible, to prove and illustrate our proposition.

THE MEMORY OF JOSEPH

Banishment from his father's home, exile, slavery, false accusations, and years in a prison could have made Joseph's lot terrible but for the alleviating power of memory. The great story makes it clear that memory was the lamp by the light of which light Joseph found his way through the dark labyrinth of his misery and unhappiness. Thomas Mann's book, *Joseph and his Brothers*, dwells at great length on the temptation of Joseph. He cites seven or eight considerations to which Joseph clung in the face of the great temptation. But the decisive thing, according to Mann's imagination, was the sudden memory that Joseph had, at the very crisis of the temptation, of his father Jacob's face. That is a beautiful fact that more tempted men than Joseph have found to be true. The angel of memory, the memory of a good father or a praying mother, the memory of a little child, or the memory of an earlier consecration, stood before the soul with drawn sword and warned it back from the path of temptation.

Not only did the memory of his father's house and his father's God keep Joseph from sin, but it kept his heart warm and tender. That is powerfully brought out in those great scenes of reconciliation when Joseph wept over his brothers until all the house of Pharaoh heard him, and again, when he wept over his father Jacob in the land of Goshen. These great Bible stories cast a light not only on our path in this world, but into the shadowy mystery of the world beyond. The immediate recognition of his brothers by Joseph, and the beautiful recognition and reunion which followed, casts a light on the relationships of the future world. Memory will be the light by which we find one another and look into one another's faces. Without memory heaven would be just an assembly of ghosts. Here we are parted for a season, that there we might have one another forever.

DAVID'S MEMORY

The most moving instance of David's memory is his recollection of Jonathan. Saul and Jonathan were long dead, fallen on the fatal field of Gilboa, and after long war between the house of Saul and the house of David, David was everywhere victorious. There was none to dispute his claim to the throne. Many would have celebrated such a victory by a wholesale massacre and proscription of their helpless foes. But what did David do in this hour of victory and triumph? He remembered not his enemies, but his friends, and said, "Is there any yet left of the house of Saul, that I may show him the kindness of God, for Jonathan his son's sake?" David remembered the beautiful and loyal friendship of Jonathan, and how at the darkest period of his life Jonathan had come to him in the Wood of Ziph and strengthened his hand in God.

Memory thus is one of the greatest and sweetest words because it inspires beautiful deeds. Some think that the Taj Mahal in India is the most beautiful building ever reared by the band of man. It was built in memory of a faithful wife. Stanford University, illustrious for its scholarship and faculty, and renowned the world over for its beautiful buildings, is a creation of memory, a father and mother's loving memory of an only son.

PAUL'S MEMORY

One thing that will always strike you in reading the letters of St. Paul is the way in which these letters, with their profound statements about the Christian doctrines, come to a conclusion, first, with practical advice for daily life, and then with greetings to old friends. Whether he was writing to the Corinthians, or the Philippians, or the Colossians, or the Romans, there is always someone whom Paul remembers with gratitude and affection. The Christians at Philippi are mentioned and remembered with particular gratitude. In the introduction to his letter to them he says, "I thank my God upon every remembrance of you."

Then there is that rosary of friendship at the end of the Letter to the Romans, where Paul salutes and mentions Ampliatus and Urbane and Herodian and Narcissus, and other disciples there with their beautiful Roman names, and then a man named Rufus, "and his mother and mine." But one of the most pleasing memories that Paul had was his memory of a Christian at the Church in Ephesus. His name was Onesiphorus. Paul hands him down to immortality as a man who came to visit him when he was in prison at Rome, and says of him that "he oft refreshed me and was not ashamed of my chains." He prays that God may give mercy unto the house of Onesiphorus, and that he may find mercy of the Lord "in that day." There is something about these references to Onesiphorus which suggest that perhaps Onesiphorus was now dead. One has imagined Paul requesting Timothy to lay a flower upon the grave of Onesiphorus.

> Timotheus, when here and there you go
> Through Ephesus upon your pastoral round,
> Where every street to me is hallowed ground,
> I will be bold and ask you to bestow
> Kindness upon one home, where long ago
> A helpmate lived, whose like is seldom found,
> And when the sweet spring flowers begin to blow,
> Sometime, for me, to lay one upon his mound.
> —Author Unknown

Enough has been said, I think, to show that memory is in truth the sweetest word. But if any doubt as to that should be left in anyone's mind, let us crown our illustration and demonstration by the example of Jesus Himself. On the same night on which He was betrayed, our Lord chose to bind Himself forever to the hearts of His disciples by the mystic chords of memory. He asked them to celebrate His death and so remember Him. "This do in remembrance of Me." We remember His words and His example and character only because we first remember His death. Thus it is that our highest and holiest hopes and desires are created and cherished by our memory of Christ as our Savior.

MEMORY AS THE MOST BITTER WORD

In one of the art galleries in Belgium there is a picture entitled "Napoleon in Hell." It represents the Emperor surrounded by the hosts of those who were slaughtered in his wars. According to the artist's conception, hell for Napoleon was the memory of those whose death he had brought about to further his ambitions. There is indeed such a thing as a remembrance of sin. There are those alive today who would give all that they possess if they could expunge from the tablets of their memory the record of an evil deed. Memory becomes the bitterest word, not at all because of the recollection of hardships of past trials or sufferings or sorrows, but because of the recollection of evil deeds. "Thou makest me to possess the sins of my youth." Thus, memory is the agent of conscience and retribution.

Who are some of the men in the Bible who were tormented with bitter memories? Among them were those cruel men, the brothers of Joseph. When on their first visit to Egypt Joseph threatened them with prison and death and compelled them to leave one of their brothers, Simon, as a hostage, the conscience of these men was awakened, and they said one to another, "We are verily guilty concerning our brother, in that we saw the anguish of his soul when he besought us, and we would not hear. Therefore is this distress come upon us. They did not yet know that it was Joseph who was talking with them and who threatened them, but memory awakened conscience and brought their great sin of the past, of the long ago, before them.

Another man who had bitter memories was that monstrous king of the Canaanites, Adonibezek. During his reign he had captured seventy kings and had amused himself by cutting off their great toes and thumbs and leaving them thus mutilated to eat the crumbs that fell from his table. When the army of Israel captured him they did to him just as he had done to those seventy kings. In his suffering and bloody mutilation, Adonibesek remembered his past transgressions and recognized the justice of the punishment and revenge which had fallen upon him. "As I have done, so God hath requited me."

Jacob was another man who had bitter memories. Long years after he had shamefully deceived and wronged his brother Esau, Jacob, now a rich man, is returning from Mesopotamia with his flocks and herds, to his own country. At the fords of the Jabbok Jacob received word that Esau was on his way to meet him, "and four hundred armed men with him." God in His mercy touched the heart of Esau, and Jacob was spared. But until the night had passed, fearful and bitter were Jacob's memories of his past despicable transgression.

Another man who had bitter memories was Peter. When he was cursing his Lord in the courtyard of the high priest, suddenly the cock crowed, and then Peter "remembered the word of the Lord," how Christ had warned him that that very night he would betray Him. When Peter thought of that he remembered all the tenderness and love and affection of his Savior, and went out into the night and "wept bitterly." I have no doubt, too, that the remorse of Judas, when he flung the blood money down before the high priests and then went out into the night and hanged himself, was the remorse created by memory.

But the most striking example of a bitter memory is that of the rich man whose fate was described by Jesus in the parable of Dives and Lazarus. While Dives and his brothers and companions sat at their well-furnished table, clothed in purple and fine linen, the beggar Lazarus lay at his gate, desiring to be fed with tile crumbs that fell from the rich man's table. Moreover the dogs came and licked his sores. That is the great contrast with which Christ starts His parable. Then comes the second contrast—two funerals. The rich man dies and is buried, and no doubt there was a great funeral as he was laid in a costly rockhewn tomb. The beggar also died and was buried. There were no mourners and no spices as he was carried to the pauper's field. But there were others there. "The beggar died and was carried by the angel into Abraham's bosom." And when the curtain rises on the scene in the next world, it is another contrast, only the roles of the rich man and the beggar are reversed. Lazarus is in the bosom of Abraham, and the rich man is in hell and in torment. When he beholds Lazarus afar off in the bosom of Abraham, the rich man asks Abraham to send Lazarus to minister to him and cool his tongue, for, he says, "I am tormented in this flame." Then comes that tremendous saying of Jesus, or rather the word he puts in the mouth of Abraham, "Son, remember!" Remember what? "Remember that thou in thy life time receivedst thy good things and likewise Lazarus evil things. But now he is comforted and thou art tormented."

Just as there could be no heaven without memory, so there can be no hell without memory, and just as memory can create a beautiful heaven, so memory can create a place of torment.

> What is this power
> That recollects the distant past
> And makes this hour,
> Unlike the last,
> Pregnant with life?
> Calling across the deep
> To things that slumber, men that sleep.
> They rise by number,
> And with stealthy creep,
> Like a battalion's tread,
> Marshall our dead.
>
> This is the gift
> Men cannot bargain with nor shift;
> Which went with Dives
> Down to hell,
> With Lazarus up to heaven;
> Which will not let us 'ere forget

The sins of years,
Though washed with tears.
Whate'er it be,
Men call it, "Memory."

—Author Unknown

Yes, memory is the sweetest word, but it is also the bitterest word. The conclusion of the whole matter is to make friends with our today, which is yesterday's tomorrow, and lay up for ourselves pleasant memories in the future. It is all summed up by what the wise man said long ago, "Remember now thy Creator," and by what St. Paul, writing from his prison in Rome, where the darkness was illuminated by beautiful memories, said to Timothy, his young disciple and friend of Ephesus, "Remember Jesus Christ." Yes, that is the thing to do, that is the way to inherit memories that will bless and not burn. Remember His example and His spirit in your daily life. Remember His mercy and His love, and His death on the Cross for your sins; and when you remember that, how God in Christ has forgiven and forgotten your sins and remembers them no more, then even the memory of your sins will be lost to you in the sweet recollection of His wondrous love and mercy.

13

THE WORD THAT
CONQUERS GOD

What mighty word is that? What word is so mighty that it can conquer God? What is the word that turns captivity captive? What is the word that unites far sundered souls around one common mercy seat? What is the word that brings man's storm-driven bark into the haven of safety and peace? What is the word that turns back the shadow of death on the face of life's dial? What is the word that giveth songs in the night, that lifts the load of guilt from the conscience-smitten heart? What is the word that puts a sword in our hand when we face temptation? What is the word that gives us strength to bear our daily burdens? What is the word that fortifies the soul when it kneels before its cup in some Gethsemane of sore agony? What is the word that lifts us up when we have fallen? What is the word that brings angels down from heaven to minister to us when we have overcome the devil? What is the word that makes us co-workers with God in the coming of His Kingdom? What is the word that recalls the wanderer from the far country? What is the word that is the best physician for both body and soul? What is the word which, when we speak it, may set a captive free? What is the word that companions the soul in its hours of loneliness, that comforts it in the day of sorrow? What is the word that sets a lamp of forgiveness and reconciliation in the window for the prodigal and the wanderer?

What is the word that brings the eternal world to view? What is the word that is the simplest form of speech that infant lips can try? What is the word that is the sublimest strain that can reach the majesty on high? What is the word that makes the angels rejoice when they hear it on the lips of a contrite sinner? What is the word that is our watchword at the gate of death, the word with which we enter heaven?

That mighty, all prevailing, God-conquering word is *prayer*. "The effectual fervent prayer of a righteous man availeth much"—James 5:16.

The word that conquers God. That is a bold thing to say, and yet we say it by the authority of none other than the greatest example in prayer Himself, our Savior Jesus Christ, who said, "Knock and it shall be opened unto you," and who told two parables, the Parable of the Midnight Visitor and the Parable of the Widow and the Unjust Judge, to encourage us in prayer and to show how prayer conquers God.

When we come to select examples and illustrations from the Bible which shall prove and demonstrate our proposition that prayer is the word that conquers God, our only embarrassment is the riches of the Bible in that respect, and our only difficulty is to decide what instances of God-conquering prayer to select.

ABRAHAM'S PRAYER

We commence with the first recorded prayer in the Bible, the prayer of Abraham for Sodom and Gomorrah. It is a striking and beautiful fact that in the Bible, which is the great treasury of prayers, the first recorded prayer—if we omit Cain's cry on his punishment, which is more an exclamation of sorrow than a prayer—is a prayer of intercession. There prayer is seen at its highest. Life's golden altar is the altar of intercession. Man never does a nobler act than when he becomes a priest to his fellow man and makes intercession for him.

As Abraham sat before his tent on the plains of Mamre, he lifted up his eyes, and lo, three men stood by him. After the men had been graciously entertained by Abraham, they gave him and his wife Sarah the promise that a son would be born unto them. Then they departed in the direction of Sodom, Abraham courteously walking part of the way with them. When the other men, to Abraham's view, were gone, and only one remained, Abraham drew near to God. He had learned who his mysterious visitor was, and he had learned that judgment was about to fall on Sodom and Gomorrah because of their great wickedness. Some men might have said, "That is what they deserve. They have had plenty of warnings and have not heeded them. Now let them perish." But that was not what Abraham thought, and not what Abraham said—noble, magnanimous Abraham, the Friend of God.

Abraham drew near to God and began to plead for the wicked cities, asking if God would not spare them for the sake of the righteous men that lived there. Abraham did not know how few righteous men were there. But drawing a bow at a venture, he commenced with fifty: "Peradventure, if there be fifty righteous within the city, wilt thou also destroy, and not spare the place for the fifty righteous that are therein? Shall not the judge of all the earth do right?" Then God promised Abraham that He would spare the city if there were fifty righteous then. Then Abraham, with beautiful humility, and yet angelic earnestness, said, "Behold now I have take upon me to speak unto the Lord, which am but dust and ashes. Wilt Thou destroy all the city for the lack of five?" And God said, "If I find there forty and five, I will not destroy it." And so Abraham continued his pleading with God, asking that the place be spared for the sake of thirty righteous, and then for the sake of twenty, and finally for the sake of ten.

Alas, not even ten righteous could be found in Sodom. Destruction and death fell upon the city and all its inhabitants, save Lot and his daughters. But there is something deeply moving, infinitely tender and pathetic, wonderfully uplifting about that intercession of the Friend of God for the wicked inhabitants of Sodom and Gomorrah. That is the way we ought to feel towards our fellow men, and that is the way we ought to approach God and to pray to Him. Who knows how much you and I owe to those who have pled with God for our souls? Go, then, to the golden altar of prayer, and there offer your prayers in behalf of other souls.

There is a place where thou canst touch the eyes
Of blinded men to instant, perfect sight;
There is a place where thou canst say, "Arise!"
To dying captives, bound in chains of night;
There is a place where thou canst reach the store
Of hoarded gold and free it for the Lord;
There is a place—upon some distant shore—
Where thou canst send the worker or the Word;
There is a place where Heaven's resistless power
Responsive moves to thine insistent plea;
There is a place—a silent, trusting hour—
Where God Himself descends and fights for thee.
Where is that blessed place—dost thou ask "Where?"
O, Soul, it is the secret place of prayer.
                    —Adelaide A. Pollard, "The Indian Christian"

JACOB'S PRAYER

Another man whose prayer conquered God was Jacob. We have the record of that conquest in one of the most mysterious transactions of the Bible. There is something about it that appeals to you because of its very inscrutable mystery, and yet something there that appeals to you because you feel there is something in it that is deeply human. I refer to Jacob's midnight encounter with the angel on the fords of the Jabbok.

It was twenty years since Jacob had deceived his dying father Isaac and cheated his brother Esau out of the blessing that belonged to the firstborn. During those two decades, although he had to struggle and fight for it, Jacob had found love, a home, and prosperity in Mesopotamia, and now, a rich man, is returning to his father's country, when suddenly there falls across his path the shadow of his old transgression. He receives word that his brother Esau is on the march to meet him, and four hundred armed men with him. Perhaps Jacob hoped that Esau was dead, or, if living, that he had forgotten his great sin against him. Now he learns that Esau is on the march to meet him, Esau the cheated and the wronged, who had sworn an oath that he would kill his brother Jacob at sight.

Although distressed and frightened, Jacob's old cunning did

not desert him. He divided his people and his flocks and herds into two bands and sent them on before him, so that if Esau attacked one company the other might escape. Then he made his prayer to God, that God would deliver him out of the hand of Esau. He then sent messengers with costly presents to Esau, hoping thus to placate his brother. Having sent his company across the ford of the Jabbok, Jacob remained himself on the other side. "And Jacob was left alone!" This was to be the greatest experience of Jacob's life. It was an experience which came to him when he was left alone. Do not fear your solitary moments. God will come closer to you then than at any other time.

As Jacob stood there, alone in the shadows, there wrestled a man with him until the breaking of the day. Who or what he was, Jacob knew not. But he did not seek to shun the battle or escape the encounter. All through the night the two antagonists fought there on the banks of the little stream. There was not a spectator to view their struggles. There was not a sound save the scuffling of their feet and the panting and labored breathing of the wrestlers. In awful solitude they fought. In the battle Jacob seemed to be getting the advantage, so much so that his mysterious antagonist touched the hollow of his thigh and put it out of joint. Yet Jacob fought on, gripping his enemy all the more fiercely and tightly.

Then, as the morning dawned, Jacob suddenly learns that this midnight wrestler is not really an enemy but a friend, and as the angel hastes to be away with the dawning of the day, Jacob grips him closely and cries, "I will not let thee go except thou bless me." Then the departing angel blessed Jacob and changed his name from Jacob, the supplanter, to Israel, prince with God, for, he said, "As a prince thou hast power with God and with men, and hast prevailed."

In that night Jacob conquered God. Mysterious though that narrative is, rich are the treasures we find in it. What opposes us in life, what makes us struggle and plant and labor is, after all, no enemy but a friend in disguise. Do not mourn over the hard and difficult experiences of life, over the touches of Providence, that, as it were, have thrown your thigh out of joint, for in ways that you know not they have made you strong. Still more is this true of our sorrows and our trials. At first they seem to come upon us with threat and anger as that mysterious battler came upon Jacob there in the lonely watches of the night on the banks of the Jabbok. But their only purpose is to bless us, change us, to teach us how to pray, and to transform our characters. Therefore, when these angels in disguise come upon you, hard though the battle is and desperate the encounter, heavy and labored though the breathing of the soul may be, make sure that you conquer God in them. Make sure that you utter the prayer of struggling Jacob, "I will not let thee go except thou bless me."

One of the noblest comments on Jacob's conquest of God that night is the poem or hymn by Charles Wesley.

> Come, O Thou Traveler unknown,
>   Whom still I bold but cannot see;
> My company before is gone,
>   And I am left alone with Thee:
> With Thee all night I mean to stay,
> And wrestle till the break of day.
>
> I need not tell Thee who I am,
>   My misery or sin declare;
> Thyself hast called me by my name—
>   Look on Thy hands, and read it there
> But who, I ask Thee, who art Thou?
> Tell me Thy name, and tell me now.
>
> Yield to me now, for I am weak,
>   But confident in self-despair;
> Speak to my heart, in blessing speak;
>   Be conquered by my instant prayer:
> Speak, or Thou never hence shalt move,
> And tell me if Thy name is Love
>
> 'Tis Love! 'tis Love! Thou diedst for me
>   I hear Thy whisper in my heart;
> The morning breaks, the shadows flee;
>   Pure, universal Love Thou art:

Thy nature and Thy name is love.
To me, to all, Thy mercies move;
—Charles Wesley

THE MOTHER WHO CONQUERED CHRIST

In the life of Christ Himself there is a beautiful and striking illustration of what He so frequently taught by parable and precept, the power of prayer to conquer God. In two of his parables, the Friend at Midnight, and how the man knocked at the door of his unwilling neighbor until he came down and gave to him, and in the Parable of the Unjust Judge who avenged the widow lest she weary Him by her continual coming, Christ taught persistence and perseverance in prayer. But in His dealing with the Syro-Phoenician mother, He Himself illustrated the power of earnest, effectual, God-conquering prayer.

On the shores of Syria where Tyre once stood you can still see the waves of the Mediterranean breaking over the prostrate pillars that once were the glory of Tyre. Standing there, one thinks of Tyre and its temples and its navies, of Nebuchadnezzar and Alexander who brought Tyre into the dust. But most of all of how a poor heart-broken mother persuaded Jesus to heal her daughter.

This woman, probably a widow, had an only child, a daughter, who was grievously afflicted with an unclean spirit. When she heard that the great healer of Israel had come to their village her heart beat high with hope. But when she spoke of the matter to her neighbors, they, no doubt, discouraged her. They probably said, "He will do nothing for you. Remember we are pagans and He is a Jew. Even if you get to where he is, his friends and disciples will not let you approach Him." But undeterred by their discouraging remarks, the woman made her appeal to Jesus, first of all, it would seem, on the street, and then at the house. "Have mercy on me," "O Lord, Thou Son of David. My daughter is grievously vexed with a devil." But what was the answer of Jesus? He answered her not a word! Nothing hurts, humiliates, and disconcerts, and sometimes angers, like silence. I make no attempt to explain this silence of Jesus, unless it was that He wanted not only to test out the faith and earnest-ness of this woman, but to encourage you and me in our prayers in those times when we pray and it seems that God is silent. His silence to Pilate and to Herod, to those who mocked Him and cursed Him, we can understand, but how could He be silent to this heartbroken mother in her distress?

That silence would have frozen hope in the minds of most mothers, but not so this mother. She followed Jesus to the house where He was being entertained. There the irritated disciples said to Jesus, "Send her away for she crieth after us." Perhaps they meant, "Lord, you might as well grant her re-quest, for if you do not, she will keep on bothering us this way." Or it may have been just a suggestion that Jesus rid them of this nuisance. Then Jesus spoke for the first time, not to the woman, but to the disciples, saying, "I am not sent but unto the lost sheep of the house of Israel. You know that my mission is to the Jews. It is not possible now for me to deal with those outside of Israel."

Then the poor woman, dropping the formal language in which she had first addressed Jesus as the Son of David, cried out, "Lord, help me!" It was as if she had said, "Lord, I realize that I am not a Jew. I know that I have no claims upon Thee, but I am a poor broken-hearted mother. Lord, help me!"

Then, for the first time, Jesus spoke to the woman herself. But what a speech it was! "Let the children first be filled, for it is not meet to take the children's bread and cast it unto the dogs." That evidently was a proverb, something like our, "Char-ity begins at home." It amounted to this, "Don't you know the proverb, woman, how it is not meet to take the children's bread and cast it to the dogs?" This, one would think, would have further humiliated and angered the woman. Had she not been likened to one of the dogs that prowl about the tables in that eastern land? But instead of being repulsed, this woman cried out the more earnestly, and with a beautiful quickness and charm of speech, "Yes, Lord, I know that's so. But, Lord, even the dogs eat of the crumbs that fall from their master's table!" Then Jesus, conquered by so wonderful a love and so invincible a faith, answered, "O woman, great is thy faith! Be it unto thee even as thou wilt!"

There were two remarkable things about the great faith of this woman and her conquering prayer. The first thing was the obstacles that her faith overcame: the handicap of her pagan race, the discouragement of her neighbors, the rude discouragement of the disciples, the strange disconcerting silence of Jesus, and her seeming humiliation at His hands when He likened her to the outcast dogs. Every conceivable obstacle was there. But she overcame them all, and today is immortal for her faith. The other remarkable thing about this faith is that it was exercised, not for herself but for another. There prayer reaches its grandest heights, when we pray for another.

We all have difficulties in the way of our prayers and our faith. There is the discouragement of the world about us, the discouragement which comes from unworthy disciples of Christ, and the silence of God when we long to hear His voice. In these moments of discouragement and in the face of these difficulties, remember that mother who conquered Jesus by her prayers. For your own sake, and still more for the sake of others, keep on praying and hold on to your faith. Remember that you wield in your prayer the mightiest power, the power that moves the hand that moves the world.

There is the old Talmudic legend of Sandalphon, the Angel of Prayer, how erect

> At the outermost gates
> Of the City Celestial he waits
> With his feet on the ladder of light.

There, serene in the rapturous throng, the angel of prayer, the breathless Sandalphon, stands listening, breathless, to sounds that ascend from below.

> From the spirits on earth that adore.
> From the souls that entreaty and implore
> In the fervor and passion of prayer
> From the hearts that are broken with losses
> And weary with dragging the crosses
> Too heavy for mortals to bear.

> And he gathers the prayers as he stands
> And they change to flowers in his hands
> Into garlands of purple and red;
> And beneath the great arch of the portal
> Through the streets of the city immortal
> Is wafted the fragrance they shed.

In this beautiful legend is embodied the truth that our prayers are never lost. God is a prayer-hearing and a prayer-answering God. He always answers. Let us be satisfied with His answers, whether or not they are the answers that we expected. Prayer is the key to the problems of our day; it locks the door that keeps out the doubts and dangers of the night. There are two prayers which we are encouraged to make, and about the answer to which there can be no doubt: one is, "Thy will be done"; the other, "God be merciful to me, a sinner." Christ heard that last prayer in His last hour on the Cross and was conquered by it, for He said to that penitent thief, "Today shalt thou be with me in Paradise."

14

THE INEVITABLE WORD

What is the inevitable word? What is the word that to each man seems unnatural when applied to himself, but natural when applied to others? What is the word that God never intended man to pronounce? What is the word that man began to speak only after he had pronounced the saddest word? What is the word that reduces all men to the same rank? What is the word that strips Dives of his millions and Lazarus of his rags? What is the word that cools avarice and stills the fires of passion? What is the word that men struggle not to pronounce, and yet all must pronounce, the prince and the peasant, the fool and the philosopher, the murderer and the saint? What is the word that none is too young to lisp and none too old or too weary to whisper? What is the word that frustrates ambition and disappoints hope, and yet a word that has the power to solve all the problems and heal all the wounds of life? What is the word that men one day shrink from, and yet on another day, and in different circumstances, desire and seek after more than hidden treasure? What is the word that men fear, and yet the word which, if men will listen to its voice, can teach them the meaning of all other words in life? That word is *death*. "It is appointed unto men once to die"—Hebrews 9:27.

> O eloquent, just, and mighty death,
> Whom none could advise, thou hast persuaded;

What none hath dared, thou but done;
And whom all the world hath flattered,
Thou only but cast out of the world and despised.
Thou but drawn together all the far stretched greatness,
All the pride, cruelty, and ambition of man,
And covered it all over with these two narrow words,
 Hie Jacet.

      —Raleigh, *History of the World*

"It is appointed unto all men once to die." Towards the end of his life Daniel Webster related how once he attended divine service in a quiet country village. The clergyman was a simple-hearted, pious old man. After the opening exercises he arose and pronounced his text, and then with the utmost simplicity and earnestness said, "My friends, we can die but once." "Frigid and weak as these words might seem," said Webster, "at once they were to me among the most impressive and awakening I ever heard." That is a striking illustration of the power of a text like this, not merely to warn men of the inevitable word and the inevitable fact, but to awaken them and to inspire them to a right kind of a life. It is with that thought in mind that in this series on "The Greatest Words in the Bible" I come tonight to the inevitable word.

It is easy to think of others having to keep this appointment with death, but difficult for us to remember that we, too, must keep that appointment. "All men think all men mortal but themselves." When we see soldiers going to the front, or read of a condemned prisoner, or visit a mortally stricken man, we are conscious of a certain solemnity which gathers about such persons. But the same solemnity gathers about us, about all men. Death is appointed for all, and the question of its occurrence is merely a matter of time. Other appointments in life, the appointments of business, or pleasure, we can neglect or break, and take the consequence. But here is an appointment that no man can neglect, that no man can break. He can meet it only once, but he must meet it once.

   The glories of our blood and state
   Are shadows, not substantial things;

There is no armor against fate;
Death lays his icy band on kings.
Sceptre and crown must tumble down,
And in the dust be equal made
With the poor crooked scythe and spade.

—James Shirley

We have but one appointment with death. If it were appointed unto men twice to die, then the first appointment would not be so important, because we might hope to correct at the second appointment what was wrong in our life and in our way of meeting death at the first appointment. But death has for each of us just one rendezvous and appointment. "It is appointed unto all men once to die."

That death is the inevitable word certainly needs no demonstration or illustration, either in the Bible or out of it. All the facts of life proclaim it. But from the lives of men whose life and death are written in the Bible, we shall show the right and the wrong way to die, how poorly or how triumphantly men keep this appointment with death.

MEN WHO DIED IN THE WRONG WAY

It is recorded of one of the kings of Judah, Jehoram, that when he died "he departed without being desired." There was a man who kept an appointment with death in the wrong way because he had lived the wrong kind of a life. Yet he was a prince who had every advantage. He had for his father one of the best of the kings of Judah, Jehoshaphat. He had for a preacher the great prophet Elijah, who warned him when he was in the midst of his wicked reign of idolatry and murder. Yet, in spite of these advantages and these warnings, Jehoram lived the life which he had chosen to live, and when at length the end came, that is the epitaph you read upon his tomb, "He departed without being desired." No one mourned him; no one regretted that for him time was no more.

In contrast with the epitaph on the grave of this young prince is that on the grave of another, "And all Israel mourned for him." This was the epitaph on the grave of Abijah.

According to the popular theories of heredity and environment, Abijah ought to have been a wicked man, for he was the son of the wicked king, that king of Israel who made Israel to sin, Jeroboam, and he was brought up in that most wicked court. And yet, in spite of that heredity and environment, he lived a beautiful life, and when that life was untimely cut off as a judgment upon Jeroboam and his wife, the whole nation felt that his passing was a calamity. All Israel mourned over him. Both of these young men lived short lives. But one does not need to live long to do great good or great evil in the world. Remember, then, those two epitaphs—"He departed without being desired," and, "All Israel mourned over him." Which will you choose?

Another man who met death in the wrong way was the handsome and gifted son of David, Absalom. As a rule, the Bible tells us very little about the death and passing of either its worst or its greatest men. But there are a few exceptions, and Absalom is one of those exceptions. The story of his death and of his father's sorrow and lamentation over him is one of the most moving passages in the Bible or out of it.

What is it that we feel and think most as we listen to that cry of David over his dead and dishonored son, "O my son, Absalom, my son! My son Absalom! Would God I had died for thee, O Absalom, my son, my son!" What we think and feel most when we hear that cry is that a life has been wasted. We think of what the gifted and accomplished son of David might have been, and what he might have done for Israel. Perhaps in David's heart, too, when he wished that he might have died in Absalom's stead, was the echo of a troubled conscience, for David must have remembered his transgressions, and that prediction of the prophet Nathan at the time of David's great sin, that the sword would never depart from his house. In David's cry, too, there was that longing for death which comes to the anguished smitten soul. When Charles Summer, the great Senator from Massachusetts, who had to drink so bitter a cup of sorrow in his own domestic life, was struck with death, there lay on his table a copy of Henry VIII, with these lines marked by his own hand—

Would I were dead! If God's good will were so;
For what is in this world but care and woe!

But deeper than all else in this cry of David over Absalom is the note of lament over a wasted life. The inevitable word had been pronounced, the inevitable hour had come, but Absalom was not ready for it. All that he left behind him was the memory of wrong deeds, and noble gifts prostituted and wasted. In the king's dale the morning sun, and the moon by night, gilded with splendor the costly tomb and monument that Absalom had built for himself. But it was a tomb without a tenant, a pillar without a prince.

Another man who met the appointed hour and the appointment with death in the wrong way was that man, and the only man, whom Jesus called a fool. He is an illustration, too, of how death keeps its appointments with us when we ourselves fancy we are the furthest away from such an appointment.

This man of whom Jesus spoke in his parable had prospered greatly in the things of this world. His only worry was how to take care of his money, how to store what he had gathered. He was busy making preparations, planning to tear down his barns and build greater, and then "take it easy" in life and enjoy what he had accumulated. "Soul," he said to himself, "thou hast much goods laid up many years. Take thine ease. Eat, drink, and be merry." That was his plan, the order of his life. But his plans had a sudden interruption. God said to him, "Thou fool, this night thy soul shall be required of thee. Then whose shall those things be which thou hast provided."

How powerful, how overwhelming is that saying of Jesus; and yet, alas, how many live just like that man, rejoicing in the things they have accumulated, and planning for further accumulation and further enjoyment, building their hope on things; and then, suddenly, all these things forever swept away. This night! The inevitable word!

MEN WHO MET DEATH'S APPOINTMENT IN THE RIGHT WAY, OR THE DEATH OF A SAINT

A man who met death's appointment in the right way, and

the story of whose death thrills us, inspires us, and comforts us, was the first martyr, Stephen. At first that appointment with death for Stephen seems so bitter and cruel and dark. He had lived nobly, courageously, had testified to Christ, and then is dragged out by his enemies and stoned to death. But when we hear what Stephen said, when we see what even his enemies saw in his face, when we see what Stephen saw with his dying vision, then we are encouraged, uplifted, and inspired to live as Stephen lived and to die with his faith.

The scene of Stephen's death is one of the most moving and inspiring in all the Bible. Stephen was a good man, full of the Holy Ghost, and had courageously testified to Christ and rebuked his enemies. His ability and his fidelity made him a mark for the enemies of Christ. The last words of Stephen were words of love and pity and forgiveness, for he prayed, ere he died, "Lord, lay not this sin to their charge." When his enemies looked on him at his death, they saw in his face "as it had been the face of an angel." Already death, the great destroyer and defiler, was transforming Stephen into the likeness of the heavenly glory, so that even his bruised and battered face seemed to have an angelic look about it!

But yet more striking and more moving was what Stephen himself saw as he died. He looked up steadfastly into heaven and saw the glory of God, and Jesus standing on the right hand of God. In his death, forsaken and stoned by men, Stephen was not forsaken by Christ. No true believer, no faithful disciple ever is. "I will never leave thee and never forsake thee." This we can count upon, that our fidelity to Christ, our obedience to His will, our testimony to His kingdom, will bring us His presence and His blessing in that inevitable appointment which we have with death.

The Psalmist said, "Precious in His sight is the death of His saints." The death of Stephen showed that to be true. But there is the death of another saint which shows us how precious in the sight of God such a death is, and which shows us how to live and how to die. It was the death of that good woman who lived and died at Lydda, and whose name was Dorcas. She is spoken of as "a woman full of good works and alms-deeds which she did." When Peter came to the house where she had died, and into the upper chamber where she lay, all the widows, all the unfortunate, stood by him in tears, each one holding up a coat or a garment which Dorcas had made for them "while she was with them."

How striking and full of deep meaning is that phrase "while she was with them." Her time to be with them was limited. But while she was with them she showed them her compassion and her pity and her love. She was gone, but here in these garments, sewn by her tireless hands, were the tokens of her faithful and loving fife.

This is Mother's Day, and thousands of sons and daughters have recalled the name and the face and the tender and sacrificial love of their mothers. When they think of her they think of her as the friends of Dorcas remembered her, "full of good works and alms-deeds which she did." Our mother's day with us was long with tender ministry and sacramental love. Like a blessed candle her life burned on through the darkness of the long night. Yet now in the struggles of life it seems so brief a time. But while she was with us, all that love and faith could suggest and inspire were done for us. When death at length came it did not seem a conquest, but a coronation, not an ending, but a new beginning. What could death do to such a life, but perpetuate it, enthrone it and crown it?

I stood one day in sanctifying memories by the side of the sainted dead. Suddenly, I was conscious of the presence of another. Turning about, I saw a stranger standing near. As he seemed to be waiting for me to speak, I said to him, "Friend, who art thou? And why dost thou intrude upon my sacred memories and reflections?" At that he answered, and with a note of impatience in his voice, "Do you not know me? I am the king of terrors!"

"The king of terrors? I see nothing terrible about thee."

"No, you see nothing terrible about me, for when men and women live and die as this woman lived and died, there I have no terrors at my command. My authority has vanished. But where men have lived in selfishness, or impurity, or strife and hatred, where they have lived for this present world and for the things of this world, and where they have lived without God and without hope, there it is that I rear my throne and dress it with such terrors as are at my command. But here I have no power and no tenors. Mortal, blessed and happy in thy memories of the sainted dead. I leave thee in peace."

From the realms of the blessed, and from the kingdom of the redeemed, faithful Christian mothers speak today to their sons and daughters and tell them how to live and how to die. In the midst of life's struggles and battles, they tell us to be strong. In the midst of life's temptations they tell us to be pure and true. In the midst of life's sorrows they comfort us with the recollection of their love and affection, and by the inevitable gateway of death they invite us to meet with them, and meet with the Lamb upon His throne, in that blessed land of the faithful, where they go no more out and come no more in, and where there shall be no more death. No! The inevitable word has given way to the eternal word, Life! Life! Life!

15

THE WORD THAT IS THE GREATEST TEACHER

Life has many great teachers. Pain is a great teacher. Death is a great teacher. Sorrow is a great teacher. Love is a great teacher. But what is the word that sums up the instruction of all other words? What is the word which is a university where all men matriculate, but where not all learn, and where not all receive a degree? What is the word that teaches you more than all the schools and colleges? What is the word that offers its wisdom, its riches, and its honors to all men, and yet by many is rejected, scorned and despised? What is the word that shows us the value of a moment of time? What is the word that proves that the way of the transgressor is hard, but that the path of the just is as a shining light? What is the word that shows the unhappiness of the life that is lived for self? What is the word that shows the worth of prayer, and proves the power of faith? What is the word that demonstrates the reward of the good life and makes it certain to us that he who casts his bread upon the waters after many days shall find it again? What is the word that tells us that life's highest satisfaction is in doing good to others? What is the word which is the only lamp by which we can judge the future? What is the word that assures us that all things work together for good to them that love God? What is the word that lets us know that this world can never satisfy the soul of man, and that God hath set eternity in our heart? What is the word that lets us know how great are the mercies of God, and how wonderful His redeeming love in Christ Jesus? That word is *experience.* "I have learned by experience"—Genesis 30:27.

The man who said this was Jacob's uncle, Laban. Jacob wanted to leave Laban and go back to his own place and his own country. But Laban tried to persuade him to remain with him. He said, "Tarry, I pray thee, for I have learned by experience that the Lord hath blessed me for thy sake." Laban was a crafty, shrewd skinflint, and his only thought in having Jacob remain with him was that he might enrich himself through Jacob's industry and ability. But even on that low plane, Laban was a wise man, for he had done what a great many fail to do—learn by experience.

Experience is the greatest teacher because it draws upon all the inexhaustible stores of knowledge that are in joy and sorrow, success and disappointment, pain and pleasure, good and evil. Experience is life, and life, of course, is the greatest teacher. Whom out of the Bible shall we select to show that this is so?

The Experience of Joseph

The experience of Joseph proves that providence is in our life, that there is a divinity that shapes our ends, that there are treasures in darkness, and that all things work together for good to them that love God. This truth, grasped by the mind, and held by faith, is one of the most important parts of armor that the victorious knight can wear. Things happen to you in life. Why do they happen? What will they do to you? What is the purpose of these events, both the good and, what seems to us, the evil. One of the greatest answers ever given was that by Joseph. His bitter experience, sold as a slave into Egypt by his own flesh and blood, falsely charged with a wicked crime, cast into prison and left to languish there for long years, was of a nature to make Joseph sour and cynical, and bitter and unbelieving. To us it would seem a hard retrospect, even from the vantage point of prosperity and affluence.

Yet, see what Joseph said of it all to his vengeance fearing brothers who came to him after the death of their father Jacob, and, thinking that now Joseph would "get even" with them, sought his pardon and his mercy. "Fear not, for am I in the place of God? But as for you, ye thought evil against me, but God meant it unto good, to bring to pass as it is this day, to save much people alive."

This was not only a striking and beautiful instance of faith in the dealings of God, but also a remarkable philosophy of life. Joseph did not mean merely that his own troubles had finally issued in prosperity and peace, but that they had enabled him to do good to others. "God meant it unto good, to save much people alive"; or, as he put it when he first disclosed himself to his brothers, "God did send me before you to preserve life." There is a noble and uplifting and inspiring thought of life, a view of life that seeks in all the events of life some plan and purpose of God to make you more fitted for doing good to others. "Be thou a blessing!" When we think of life in that way, every relationship of life, every duty, and every experience is sanctified and made radiant with imperishable light.

SOLOMON'S EXPERIENCE

The experience of Solomon proves that there is no lasting satisfaction or joy in the things of this world. Solomon was a man of wide experience, not only as to wives, but as to the affairs of life. He was a man of vast erudition and knowledge. He knew all the trees and plants, and their names, from the cedar of Lebanon to the hyssop that springeth out of the wall. He was a great author and maker of proverbs. He was a great builder, and for centuries the beautiful temple at Jerusalem was a monument to his power and genius as a builder. In the Book of Ecclesiastes he tells of his experiment in the things of this world. First of all he tried pleasure. He said to his heart, "Go to now, I will prove thee with mirth. Therefore enjoy pleasure." But the result of all that was, "This is also vanity." Then he tried dissipation and gave himself, he says, unto wine. And this was his verdict, "Wine is a mocker, strong drink is raging." Then he experimented with great works. He erected great buildings. He tried his hand at agriculture, planting vineyards, gardens, orchards and building reservoirs of water. But there was no satisfaction in that. Then he experimented to see what there was in gathering gold and silver from all the provinces of his kingdom until he was the greatest king that ever reigned. Indeed, he tells us he tried everything that his mind could think of or his heart could desire, and this was his verdict: "Vanity and vexation of spirit, and there was no profit under the sun." This almost turned him into a cynic, and he tells us that he hated life because it had so mocked him and deceived him.

But this does not mean that for Solomon life was a failure. His vast experiment in building, writing books, planting, accumulating, tilling the soil, in drinking and in pleasure, in dancing men and women, ended in the discovery that this was the conclusion of the whole matter, and the whole duty of man: "Fear God and keep His commandments." The world is a great world, but it is a world that mocks and deceives unless it be morally and spiritually interpreted, unless we deal with it, not as an end, but a means, not as a final thing, but as a probation for higher things and a higher world.

THE PRODIGAL'S EXPERIENCE

Christ told an eternal tale when He told the parable of the Prodigal Son. The Prodigal Son's experience demonstrates the truth that man seems so unwilling to learn, that the way of the transgressor is hard. You know the story well. This young man wanted to have his fling in life. God gave him the desire of his heart, but sent leanness to his bones. His expedition into the far country came to an end with a job as a keeper of swine. There he sat, stripped of his money, stripped of his fine clothing, stripped of his honor and his self respect, and as he heard the greedy munching of the hogs, he fain would have filled his belly with the husks which the swine did eat. Was there ever such a picture of disillusionment and the deceitfulness of sin as this masterpiece from the hand of Jesus Christ Himself!

There are two things to observe and remember as we look at this ragged, disconsolate man, seated there near the swine. One is that young men and young women are not the only ones who take a trip into the far country of vice and sin. By no means! One of the saddest things of my experience as a minister is to see those who are well along in life doing the same thing, making the same tragic experiment. Frequently I see an old man walking up and down the streets near this church, who even in his wreckage shows something of a former standing and character. Not many years ago he lived in a fine house, was highly respected. Now he wanders down the street, stopping the passersby asking them for a nickel or a dime. I once buried a man well along in years, who for almost fifty years was a faithful and useful employee in an important post in one of the great corporations. In three months after he was retired and began to live on his pension, he plunged into excess, journeyed to the far country, and was picked up dead under suspicious circumstances. The great parable of Christ warns everyone of every age.

The second observation is this. When a man lets go morally, he always ends in the companionship of the swine. That doesn't mean that you will see him as a ragged man, or a dirty unkempt fellow, rubbing up against you on the street to panhandle you. But always his inner companions are swinish. That is all that sin does for a man.

But thank God, the story of this lost son and the experience through which he passed teaches more than that the way of the transgressor is hard. It teaches that the way of repentance is the way to happiness and to peace. Generally, we devote most of our time in commenting on the Prodigal Son to a description of his outward journey. But let us not forget the homeward journey. Follow him in your imagination as he takes his way homeward again, passing through the same towns and villages where he had had his fling on the outward journey, driven away now from the door when he stopped at the house of one of his old companions when he had had plenty of money. Yet ragged and famished, perhaps having to stop here and there by the way and get his living as a keeper of swine again, he stuck to his journey, until at length he reached his father's house. And when his father saw him afar off he ran and fell on his neck and kissed him. Thus by experience that lost son learned the marvelous patience and kindness and forgiving love of God. That is the greatest experience that any soul can have, so great that God sent His Son to die on the Cross to make it possible for us, so great that when it happens the angels of heaven rejoice over it.

PAUL'S EXPERIENCE

What is the final summary of Paul's grand thinking and believing, of his heroic battling in life? It is this: "Now abideth these three, faith, hope, and love." The experience of Paul taught him, and teaches you and me, that the abiding and permanent things are not what they seem, and what men commonly seek after, but are these: faith, hope, and love.

Paul names faith first of all. None who had had the experience of faith ever doubted its value. By faith Paul means no vague belief in God or a hear-after, but faith in Jesus Christ as the only Savior from sin. Time took many things from Paul in that comparatively brief but tempestuous life of his, but faith endured to the end, and his last word almost was this, "I know in whom I have believed."

Then comes hope. When Pandora, according to the ancient myth, overcome by curiosity, opened the box which the gods had given to her, every conceivable misfortune and disease and sorrow and curse made their escape and went out to afflict the children of men. When she got the lid back on the box only hope remained in it. That was the tribute the ancients paid to hope. But Paul is speaking of Christian hope. In another passage he says that "tribulation worketh experience, and experience hope, and hope maketh not ashamed." But that can never be said of the experience of the world. What it works is disillusionment and sadness and disappointment, sometimes bitterness and despair.

> The worldly hope men set their hearts on,
> Turns ashes—or it prospers; and anon,
> Like snow upon the desert's dusty face,
> Lighting a little hour or two, is gone.
> —Omar Khayyam, "Rubaiyat"

But the more experience we have of the Christian life, the

more experience we have of Christ, the greater our hope is. There, and there only, experience worketh hope. He who follows Christ faithfully is always ready to say in those words which John Bunyan puts into the mouth of Mr. Standfast, just when he was about to go down into the river—a passage which is one of the noblest in English prose—"I have loved to hear my Lord spoken of, and wherever I have seen the print of His shoe in the earth there I have coveted to set my foot, too. His name has been to me as a civet box, yea, sweeter than all perfumes. His voice to me has been most sweet, and his countenance I have more desired than they that have most desired the light of the sun."

But the greatest of these three, says Paul, is love. That does not mean that, in itself, love is greater than faith or greater than hope, but that love is the destination, the goal, to which our faith and our hope conduct us and inspire us. There will come a time when we shall no longer need faith, for we shall walk by sight and not by faith. There will come a time when we shall no longer need hope, for everything we have hoped for shall have come to pass. But there will never come a time when love shall pass away. Love is the best definition of heaven, and where love dwells, love for God and love for man, there is heaven.

> If all who hate would love us,
> And all our loves were true,
> The stars that swing above us
> Would brighten in the blue.
>
> If neighbor spake to neighbor,
> As love demands of all,
> The rust would eat the saber
> The spear stay on the wall.
>
> Then every day would glisten,
> And every day would shine,
> And God would pause to listen
> And life would be divine.
> —James Newton Matthews

JOHN'S EXPERIENCE

The experience of John taught him, and teaches us, that the world is not worth loving. The world passes away and those who love the world. Only those who love God and do His will abide forever.

But one says, "Why quote St. John, a simple fisherman who became a Christian disciple? What did John know of the world, its riches, its fame, its splendor, its pleasure. But remember that John spent the last half of his life in the midst of one of the world's greatest and most beautiful cities, the city of Ephesus, famed for its avenues, its temples, its stadium and amphitheater, its commerce and trade, and its market places where everything was sold, from horses and cattle and fine linen and gold and silver and precious stones to the "souls of men." John had a good opportunity to see how much there was or how little, in love for the world, and this was his final verdict—"The world passeth away."

I can imagine John being carried on his cot on a spring evening into the upper chamber where the disciples of Christ are met together. Looking from the windows of this upper chamber, you can see over the city of Ephesus. Yonder, to the west, is the harbor full of galleys, and the ships with their crimson sails touched to splendor by the sinking sun. Yonder, to the east, is the market place and the theater. Alongside this house where John and his friends sit runs the famous Corso, over whose white stones you can walk today, just as John and his companions did nineteen hundred years ago. And yonder in the distance rises the world renowned temple of Diana, with its glorious jasper columns. And what is that sound that the evening wind, blowing from the south, carries into this assembly of Christians? It is the shout and roar of the multitude at the amphitheater. These were the surroundings of St. John when he wrote this message. On the aged and serene face of the Apostle of love there is a sunset light more beautiful than that which gilds yonder Aegean and turns it into a sea of glass, mingled with fire. It is the light of Christian love and faith. At the evening time it shall be light. John has been dictating his letter, and it is during one of those pauses that he and his friends hear the shout and roar of the mob in the amphitheater. Then John gives the signal to his amanuensis to write, and this is what he says: "Love not the world, neither the things that are in the world, for the world passes away and the lust thereof, but he that doeth the will of God abideth forever."

Here, then, we bring this sermon on the Word that is the Greatest Teacher to a close, and here we bring to a conclusion this series of sermons on "The Greatest Words in the Bible and in Human Speech." Speaking through the men and women of the Bible, we have uttered great words and struck great chords in the heart of man. But all these words, all that they warn us from, all that they invite and woo us to, are summed up in that last message of Christ's aged disciple who leaned on His breast at the Supper, and who knew the mind of Christ: Love not the world. It passes away. Love God, live for Him, and do His will. He who does that abideth forever.

OTHER BOOKS BY CLARENCE E. MACARTNEY

Chariots of Fire

Drawing upon colorful yet lesser-known characters of the Old
and New Testaments, Dr. Clarence Macartney presents
eighteen powerful and timeless sermons. One of America's
greatest biographical preachers, Macartney's sermons aim for
the common heart of human experience. Each sermon contains
a wealth of illustrations and quotations that add depth and
insight to the exposition. *Chariots of Fire* is eye-opening, biblical
exposition from one of America's premier preachers and makes
an inspiring devotional or study resource.

ISBN 0-8254-3274-x   **192 pp.**   **paperback**

Great Women of the Bible

A collection of sermons from a master pulpiteer of yesterday.
Macartney's unique descriptive style brings these women of
the Bible to life and provides inspirational reading for all
Christians.

ISBN 0-8254-3268-5   **208 pp.**   **paperback**

Greatest Texts of the Bible

This collection of sermons represents some of the author's strongest and most impassioned preaching. Except for slight modifications and updating, and the insertion of Scripture references where needed, these sermons are reissued in their original form.

ISBN 0-8254-3266-9   **208 pp.**   **paperback**

He Chose Twelve

This careful study of the New Testament illuminates the personality and individuality of each of the Twelve Disciples. A carefully crafted series of Bible character sketches including chapters on all the apostles as well as Paul and John the Baptist.

ISBN 0-8254-3270-7   **176 pp.**   **paperback**

Paul the Man

Macartney delves deeply into Paul's background and heritage, helping twentieth-century Christians understand what made him the pivotal figure of New Testament history. Paul, the missionary and theologian, is carefully traced in this insightful work.

ISBN 0-8254-3269-3   **208 pp.**   **paperback**

Strange Texts but Grand Truths

Drawing upon seventeen striking and unusual texts of Scripture, Dr. Clarence Macartney utilizes the natural curiosity aroused by the unfamiliar to expound the important and practical truths of God's Word. Macartney brings to life overlooked lessons from biblical passages. Each sermon contains a wealth of illustrations and quotations that add depth and insight to the exposition of one of America's premier preachers, making this volume an inspiring devotional or study resource.

ISBN 0-8254-3272-3   **192 pp.**   **paperback**

Twelve Great Questions About Christ

Macartney addresses commonly asked questions about the life and person of Jesus Christ. The integrity of the Scriptures underlies the provocative answers that Dr. Macartney provides in this thoughtful book. The broad range of subject matter will inform and inspire laymen and clergy alike.

ISBN 0-8254-3267-7   **160 pp.**   **paperback**

Available from Christian Bookstores, or

kregel
PUBLICATIONS

P. O. Box 2607 • Grand Rapids, MI 49501